I Saw Your
Future
and
He's
Not
It

# About the Authors

**Louise Helene** (Illinois) is a second-generation psychic, Tarot card reader, and spiritual advisor who has been in the field for over 30 years. She was only 12 years old when she performed her first psychic reading at the urging of her mother, Spiritualist minister and psychic radio-show host Reverend Louise Helene. Louise learned her craft by helping her mother run a successful psychic advisor business, and today she has her own following of loyal clients who praise her accuracy, compassion, and humor.

**Kim Osborn Sullivan, PhD** (Illinois), is a writer and teacher, in addition to being Louise Helene's niece. She grew up in awe of the crystal ball her grandmother used for psychic readings and now loves seeing it in her aunt's office. Kim writes both fiction and nonfiction books for children and adults. She has also spent more than 15 years in the classroom teaching college students.

# I Saw Your Future

# and

# He's

# Not

# It

A Psychic's Guide to True Love

## Louise Helene

with Kim Osborn Sullivan, PhD

Llewellyn Publications
Woodbury, Minnesota

FIRST EDITION
First Printing, 2013

Book design by Donna Burch
Cover design by Lisa Novak
Cover illustration © Bunky Hurter
Edited by Andrea Neff
Part Page art © Art Explosion

Llewellyn Publications is a registered trademark of Llewellyn Worldwide Ltd.


**Library of Congress Cataloging-in-Publication Data**
Helene, Louise, 1959-
  I saw your future and he's not it : a psychic's guide to true love / by Louise Helene
with Kim Osborn Sullivan. — 1st ed.
       p. cm.
  ISBN 978-0-7387-3493-4
1. Love—Miscellanea. 2. Dating (Social customs)—Miscellanea. 3. Mate selection
—Miscellanea. I. Sullivan, Kim Osborn, 1965- II. Title.
  BF1729.L6H36 2013
  646.7'7—dc23
                          2012028543

Llewellyn Worldwide Ltd. does not participate in, endorse, or have any authority
or responsibility concerning private business transactions between our authors and
the public.
  All mail addressed to the author is forwarded, but the publisher cannot, unless specifically instructed by the author, give out an address or phone number.
  Any Internet references contained in this work are current at publication time,
but the publisher cannot guarantee that a specific location will continue to be main-
tained. Please refer to the publisher's website for links to authors' websites and
other sources.

Llewellyn Publications
A Division of Llewellyn Worldwide, Ltd.
2143 Wooddale Drive
Woodbury, MN 55125-2989
www.llewellyn.com


Printed in the United States of America

## DEDICATION

For the late Reverend Louise Helene Osborn,
beloved mother and grandmother

# Acknowledgments

The best part of having a big family is that holidays are a raucous blast. The second best part is that whenever you've got something going on in your life, there are plenty of people eager to lend a hand. Whether you're planning a wedding or going to the Renaissance Faire or even writing a book, you're not alone. So when we needed help with our book, the advantages of a large family came through loud and clear. Plenty of relatives stepped up and volunteered to review the "beta version" of the manuscript before we sent it off into the world. Thanks to Alan, Amanda, Chris, Donna, Linda, Natalie, and Veronica. They all offered valuable insights that helped improve this book. We also owe a debt of gratitude to Annmarie, who shared her talent for naming books with us.

Another advantage of having a big family is that we had lots of names to choose from to plug into the stories in this book. We borrowed names from brothers, sisters, nieces, nephews, aunts, uncles, and cousins in order to maintain confidentiality for the psychic clients whose stories are discussed in the book. Thanks to everyone who let us use their names.

Finally, huge thanks to Llewellyn for publishing this book and to our extraordinary editor Amy Glaser for pulling our manuscript out of the slush pile and helping us through the publication process. It's hard for authors to imagine anyone being as dedicated to their book's success as they are, but that's exactly how it felt when we found the right editor and publishing house. We're so grateful for the support and enthusiasm they've given us.

# Contents

## Section Four: Bad Love

# Introduction

"Please help me, Louise! Please, I can't live without him!" On the other end of the phone, Dawn dissolved into tears.

I felt a tug in my chest. It was clear that Dawn was in pain, which didn't make my job any easier. I needed to get through to her, and just sympathizing wouldn't cut it.

"Now, Dawn, stop crying. I feel that Leo cares about you, but you've got to give him a little space. You have to stop following him, because he knows what you're doing and thinks he's being stalked. He's very perceptive and aware of his surroundings."

"What!" Dawn cried. "I never follow him!"

"Maybe you can say that to other people, but I'm the psychic. I know the truth. You 'accidentally' ran into him ten times in two days. He told you he wanted to think about things, so let him think. You don't want to drive him away."

There was a pause. Then Dawn said, "So let me get this straight." Her voice had turned indignant. I knew what was coming. "You're saying that if things don't work out between us, then it's *my* fault?"

"Not your fault, sweetie. I didn't say that," I replied gently. "But it could drive him away."

"How dare you? You'll see! The two of us will be together, and it won't be any thanks to you!" After a few choice words, the line went dead. All I could do was stare at the receiver and hope that I had given Dawn something to think about before she ruined any shot she had with Leo.

After more than thirty years as a psychic advisor, I've talked to hundreds of women like Dawn and fielded thousands of questions about relationships. In fact, nine out of ten questions that I hear are about love. Why so much interest in one topic? Maybe because loving and being loved are basic human needs, but we often feel powerless when it comes to meeting those needs. People are frustrated by their inability to find the right person or to hold on to the person they want. We have control in other aspects of our lives, but we simply can't force another person to love us. As a result, people crave advice from someone who has special insight and can help eliminate some of the uncertainty. That's why millions of Americans reach out to psychics every year.

The hardest part of my job is seeing rational people driven to irrational behavior by love. Like Dawn, many people who are reasonable, law-abiding, and responsible in every other aspect of their lives can lose their perspective when it comes to matters of the heart. How can you blame them? At school or work or in financial matters, there's an obvious cause-and-effect relationship between your actions and the result. If you study for a test, you get an A. If you work hard, you get a raise. If your credit score is good, you get a low interest rate. But when it comes to love, you can do everything right, but still not catch the eye of the person you want. It's no wonder people are desperate for help.

# Psychic Readings 101

A *psychic reading* is the term used for a meeting between a psychic and client designed to answer questions about the client's past, present, or future. Psychics use a variety of methods to conduct readings, and each psychic has his or her own preferences. Common methods include Tarot cards, crystal balls, tea leaves, and astrological charts. My preferred tools are Tarot cards and sometimes a crystal ball.

When a client calls or visits me for a psychic reading, I begin by getting the client's name and birthday. Then I ask whether the client is concerned about a particular problem. The vast majority of concerns relate to love and relationships.

While the client describes the situation, I shuffle my deck of Tarot cards. Discussing the issue while shuffling the cards allows them to fall into the right order for each client. As I talk to the client, I pull cards from my Tarot deck and interpret their meanings. Based on what the cards say, I ask follow-up questions or share insights.

Occasionally I experience what I call a "psychic flash," in which I see a picture in my mind that sheds light on the issue being raised by my client. Sometimes the flash comes in the form of being able to understand, or channel, another person's thoughts. This is particularly helpful because when I know what another person is thinking, I know how to deal with that person. Sometimes a picture of a person, place, or thing pops into my mind. For instance, a client of mine recently asked if her boyfriend was cheating. I saw a sudden image of a pretty blond woman. The client had her answer. It turned out to be her guy's ex-girlfriend, who had come back to town.

The example of the blond woman brings us to the unfortunate fact that the results of a psychic reading aren't always what a client wants to hear. Please understand that I believe in love, and I want everyone to experience love, which is why I wrote this book. But sometimes love with a particular person isn't meant to be. Or, as I like to say, it's not in the (Tarot) cards. That's why some of the anecdotes in this book demonstrate how to know when you shouldn't pursue a particular romance. Those situations are painful, but the fact is that when you don't get what you want, it's always because a higher power is trying to either protect you or steer you toward something better down the road.

## The Psychic Edge

I've spent many years talking to people about the true nature of their relationship problems. My clients tell me things that they're too embarrassed to admit to their friends or psychiatrists, because with me there's an element of anonymity. Whether we're conducting the reading on the phone or face to face, my clients can use false names and change details of their lives in order to avoid being identified. They can't do that with a doctor, who has their insurance information, or with friends whom they've known for years.

Because clients know that whatever they say to me won't get back to anyone else, they feel comfortable opening up. They tell me what they've done, what's been done to them, and what they really desire. I've learned a great deal about human nature through giving readings, and I've identified the recurring issues that plague people's relationships, regardless of their age, sex, race, or culture.

I think of the special insight that psychics provide as the "psychic edge." It's the ability to see beyond the surface and pick up on the subtle whispers of intuition. With the psychic edge, it's possible to better understand what others are thinking or doing, and to know whether you're with the right person for you. Without it, you may find yourself simply fumbling in the dark when it comes to relationships. And no one wants to fumble in the dark—unless it's with a willing partner, that is. So that's the purpose of this book: It's a tool to help you avoid the frustration and uncertainty that come with finding love. And it may just guide you toward the right person to fumble in the dark with.

Since I've spent decades developing my psychic insight, you might wonder how you can gain an edge just by reading a book. Don't worry, you don't have to spend the next thirty years conducting psychic readings. The fact is that it's more difficult to see into someone else's destiny than it is to understand your own. Most people have the ability to understand what's happening in their own lives if they only know how to listen and take the time to try. That's what I'm here to teach you.

This book is broken down into the recurring themes that consistently emerge during readings with my clients. Those include such topics as why a man doesn't call, why he won't commit, and how to know when it's time to call it quits. In each section, I offer anecdotes taken directly from my readings with clients. The anecdotes include details about the clients' problems and the advice I offered, although names and other identifying characteristics have been changed to maintain anonymity. Often, I also provide information about how the situations were resolved, thanks to the fact that I have a loyal client base that provides me with follow-ups and feedback on our readings. In each chapter, activities and tools are offered that enable readers to become their own psychic advisors. Regardless of your particular needs or situation, it's possible to uncover your own insight and apply it in your life.

## ESPECIALLY FOR WOMEN

Only about 10 percent of my clients are men. Does this mean that women need more relationship help than men? The short answer is yes, because too many women mistakenly believe they have less power in romantic relationships than men do. It's easy to see how they reach that conclusion. Although times are changing, tradition still dictates that the man usually makes the first move and asks a woman out. The man decides whether to call the next day. The man proposes marriage when he's ready. When all these factors are added together, it might seem like the man gets to guide the relationship while the woman stares at her phone and wonders what's going on in her guy's head.

But it doesn't have to be that way. This book is about empowering women to understand that they're equal partners in finding and maintaining the loving relationships they deserve. That's the advantage offered by psychic insight. For years, my clients have enjoyed the edge that psychic insight offers, and their romantic lives are better for it. It allows them to better understand what their men are thinking and how to react in order to achieve the desired result. This book does the same thing for readers by showing them how to tap into their own psychic insights to shed light on their love lives. It levels the playing field and helps women realize that the control is in their hands, where it belongs.

## Meet the Authors

Another reason that this book is designed for women is that I'm a woman, so I understand your troubles. I'm a second-generation psychic, Tarot card reader, and spiritual advisor who has been in the field for more than thirty years. I was only twelve years old when I performed my first psychic reading at the urging of my mother, Spiritualist minister and psychic radio-show host Reverend Louise Helene. I learned my craft by helping my late mother run a successful psychic advisor business, and I adopted her professional name after she retired. Today I conduct most of my readings over the telephone, since that format allows me to reach people around the world who need my help. My many loyal clients praise the accuracy of my readings and my compassion and humor.

My co-author is my niece, Kim Osborn Sullivan. She's a writer and teacher who grew up in awe of the heavy crystal ball that my mother used for psychic readings. Kim has published nonfiction books, novels, and academic articles, and has spent years working as a college instructor. She has a twisted fascination with statistics, facts, and supporting data, which made her perspective especially helpful in the research sections.

Finally, I don't want to leave you wondering what happened with Dawn from the beginning of this introduction. I'm pleased to report that Dawn called me a week later to apologize. She'd needed to cool down, and when she did, she gave serious thought to what I'd said. She thought about how she'd behaved with Leo. She also recalled how scared she'd felt several years earlier when one of her ex-boyfriends had followed her and called incessantly. So she decided to give

Leo the space he'd asked for. After a week of not seeing him or following him or calling him, he called her. He wanted to get together for dinner.

By picking up this book, you've taken the first step to seizing control of your romantic relationships. Together we'll put the psychic edge to work for you.

## SECTION ONE

# Finding Love

## CHAPTER I

# Where Are All the Good Men?

Before you can fall in love and live happily ever after, you've got to find that special person who gets your motor running. Considering how hard that can be, it might seem like a miracle that anyone ever falls in love. But it's not impossible. The world is full of good single men who could be perfect for you. You just have to be able to spot them when they come along.

## ROSIE

I'll never forget the first time I spoke with Rosie. She'd been through a string of bad relationships and was at the end of her rope. The "Porno King" had been her last boyfriend. Instead of taking her out or spending time with her, he preferred to sit at home by himself watching free porn on his computer. He sent her a text message every night telling her, "Sleep tight, baby."

After she finally dumped His Majesty, Rosie decided to try online dating. Unfortunately, she didn't get any responses to her first profile—not a single one. I told her that I felt she needed to change her bio and the description of what she wanted in a man.

"My profile's so long because of all the losers I've dated," she explained. "It has to have a list of all the things I'm definitely not willing to put up with."

I warned her not to start with the negative, because it creates bad energy. "Be positive," I told her. "Stay focused on what you want, not what you don't want. If you do, you'll get more responses than you can handle."

"Okay, I'll change my profile," she agreed. "But if I do what you tell me, how long will it be before Mr. Wonderful comes into my life?"

"Not right away. I feel that you'll need to wait at least two months for the right one. You're going to sift through lots of frogs before you find your prince, but he's out there."

Then the frogs started rolling in.

Rosie began to call me twice a week to ask about the various men she'd met through the dating site, but each one was worse than the last. I found myself warning her away from all of them, which didn't make her happy.

"Why can't I meet a decent man?" she moaned week after week.

"Just be patient," I told her. "The right man is coming, but you can't rush it."

Then I didn't hear from Rosie for a couple of weeks in a row, and I began to worry. I could feel that something wasn't right.

When she finally called, she told me the story of Eddie, a man she'd met online. Because I had been so negative about all the men she'd been meeting, she hadn't called me to talk about him when they started going out. Instead, she had decided to go for it on her own. After all, she figured that her prince was just around the corner and, as she put it, "I couldn't wait any longer."

Eddie told Rosie that he was in the military and wanted to fly out to see her, but his bank was in another state where he'd done his basic training. Could she possibly wire him the money for airfare and he would pay her back when he arrived? Happily, she sent him $400. Then she waited for him at the airport. When his flight arrived, he wasn't on it. Not sure if she should be heartbroken or terrified that something had happened to Eddie, Rosie went home and tried to reach him. She left messages on his phone, but he didn't call her back.

Three days later, Eddie called. He told her that he'd been so excited about seeing her that he'd forgotten to take his insulin injection on the morning he was flying out to meet her. He had passed out in the cab on the way to the airport and had to be hospitalized. Because he had missed his flight, he lost his nonrefundable ticket. After his near-death experience, he wanted to see her even more than before. Could she possibly wire him some more money until he got his paycheck?

Rosie told me that she'd had some misgivings about Eddie's story, but she pushed them aside and sent him another $400. Again, Eddie failed to arrive on his flight. He also didn't answer her phone calls, except the one time when she blocked her phone number so he couldn't see who was on the line. That time, he hung up as soon as he realized it was her.

After all this happened, it took Rosie a few days to work up the courage to call me. She was embarrassed to admit the mess she had gotten herself involved in, but she had a lot of questions. In the end, curiosity won out over humiliation.

"All right, Louise, please be brutally honest. What do you think about what happened? And will I ever get my money back?"

"You already know the answers to those questions," I said. "First, kiss that money goodbye and consider it the cost of learning a valuable lesson. Second, never ever send money to any stranger over the Internet again. And third, please be patient! The right man is coming."

"But why does this have to be so hard?" she moaned.

"Let's try another approach. Have any new men contacted you lately from that dating website?" I asked.

"There've been some, but I haven't gotten back to any of them. I've been so distracted with Eddie, and now I'm afraid that every guy out there is just trying to take advantage of me."

I could certainly understand Rosie's reluctance to get back up on the horse, but she needed to take the right actions if she was going to get what she wanted.

"You could give up now, Rosie, but if you hang in there a little longer, the man for you is on his way. Why don't you read me the names of the men who've sent you messages lately?"

Rosie started reading the list, and when she got to Dan's name, I stopped her.

"I've got a feeling about this guy," I said. "Why don't you contact him? But be careful and take it slow. And no matter what, don't send him any money!" Rosie laughed and promised to do what I said.

The next time Rosie called me, she had much better news to report than after her fiasco with Eddie. This new guy, Dan, was the real deal. She told me that after she sent him a message, Dan wrote back right away. They communicated back and forth like that for a while, then started talking on the phone. She didn't rush it, and even told him she needed more time when he asked to have dinner together after the first week. In the end, they waited two months before meeting in person.

Dan was a firefighter paramedic, a tall, strong, romantic guy. Rosie told me he was everything she wanted in a man, but she hadn't paid any attention to him when he first contacted her on the dating site because she was so upset about Eddie. The two of them are now happily living together and talking about their future.

## Lessons Learned

We want what we want when we want it. For many women, that means they want a good man and they want him now. They're unwilling to wait. But the universe doesn't recognize people's demands. Things will happen when they're supposed to, and kicking, screaming, or fighting won't make them go faster. So if you're wondering why you can't find a good man, maybe it's simply because it's not the right time for him to arrive in your life yet. Maybe there are other things you need to deal with first, or things he needs to straighten out in his life in order to clear the road for your relationship. Regardless, patience is key. And desperation results in lousy decisions.

Rosie waded through a sea of frogs before she finally found her prince, but because of her impatience, she almost passed him by.

## JUST THE FACTS

Psychopathy is a personality disorder in which people lack empathy and guilt and the ability to foresee the consequences of their actions. As children, psychopaths tend to lie and abuse animals. They are often charming on the surface, so they blend in with society. Many people mistakenly believe that all psychopaths are bloodthirsty serial killers like Ted Bundy, John Wayne Gacy, or Dexter, but most don't exhibit such extreme behavior. Robert Hare, emeritus professor of psychology at the University of British Columbia and creator of the standard tool for diagnosing psychopathy, estimates that psychopaths make up 1 percent of the population. Not surprisingly, prisons contain a high percentage of psychopaths.

There's a difference of opinion in the field of psychology about what separates a sociopath from a psychopath. They have similar characteristics, and the terms are often used interchangeably. However, some mental health professionals believe that sociopaths acquire their disorder due to environmental factors like a traumatic childhood, while psychopaths are simply born, not made.

Many people believe that humans have an innate ability to detect psychopaths. You might get a "creepy vibe" from a person, or your friends might say that something doesn't seem quite right about your new guy. This book is all about teaching you to listen to your intuition, and this is a prime example of how it should work.

In Rosie's case, it's unclear whether her con-man Eddie was a full-fledged psychopath or not. He'd have to undergo a battery of psychological tests to figure out if he felt guilty about stealing $800 from a lonely woman. But regardless of his diagnosis, Eddie was a bad guy. Rosie's intuition was telling her so when she was embarrassed about discussing the relationship with me and when she had misgivings about sending him cash.

I understand that you're eager to find someone special, and you figure that rewards don't come without risk. However, letting yourself get involved with a psychopath—or even just a common, everyday jerk—is too big a risk. The human brain has evolved over millennia to keep us safe from predators. We don't fully understand how it does what it does, but when it sends up a red flag, it's important to pay attention. If a situation seems wrong, it probably is.

## ROBIN AND MARCUS

"I need help bad, Louise," Robin told me as soon as I picked up the phone. "I got man troubles."

I started shuffling my cards and put a few on the table. "Hmmm, I'm not sure I'd call it trouble, Robin," I said. "How about you tell me what's bothering you."

"Well, there's this man at work. Marcus is his name. He's new, only worked there a couple months. Anyway, I never gave him the time of day because I thought he was married."

I looked down at my cards and scratched my head. They didn't add up to what Robin was telling me. "So you're saying that you're getting involved with a married man?" I asked.

"No, I wouldn't do that!" Robin cried. "I got standards!"

"Of course you do. I'm sorry, I'm just confused because I don't see a wife here with this guy. Why do you think he's married?"

"That's just it. I don't think so anymore. He's got this picture of a woman and a baby on his desk, so I thought it was his family. Then last Friday he asked me to go out for a drink after work, just him and me, you know. So I said no and that he ought to be ashamed of asking me out. When he asked why, I said I don't waste my time with married men."

"And he told you he's not married," I said.

"Right. The picture's his sister and her little boy."

"Well, from what I'm seeing, he's telling the truth. Do you like this guy?"

"I sure do. You don't come across a fine man like him very often. He went to college and now he's thinking about getting his master's. He works out and owns his own house."

"He sounds perfect," I told Robin. "But since you're calling me, there must be a problem somewhere."

Robin laughed nervously. "Don't you always know, Louise? Yeah, there is something I need to know about. I need to find out if he's gonna be able to, you know, meet my expectations, if you know what I mean."

"Your expectations?" I asked. Usually I could get a good feeling about where a client was headed with a particular question, but this time I was lost.

"Yeah, my expectations. My *needs*." Robin paused, then tried again. "Marcus and me, we haven't been to bed together yet. You know, we work together, so I don't want to do that if it's not gonna work out."

"Do you want to sleep with him?"

"Oh, yeah! I told you he was fine, didn't I? But I dated a couple of guys who were, you know, too *small* down there. We had to break up because I couldn't take their little U-boats seriously."

"And you want to know if Marcus is more like a dinghy or an ocean liner?" I asked, finally catching on.

"You got it! I don't want nothin' small down there. I want the Titanic! And don't you worry. I'll know what to do with it when I get it!"

I chuckled and resisted the urge to glance into my crystal ball. I was afraid of what I might see. Then I said, "Robin, don't you worry. I can feel that you're going to be very satisfied with Marcus."

## LESSONS LEARNED

Everyone wants something different in a mate, which is ideal. If every woman were searching for a man with the same characteristics, we'd all be fighting over the same guy. Robin was lucky because she knew what she wanted—and, in her own words, she'd "know what to do with it" when it came along.

She wanted me to tell her about Marcus's size, but that wasn't necessary. I could see that the two of them were suited to each other, which automatically meant that she'd be satisfied with him. Whether he was the Titanic or not, I felt that she'd be happy. Plus, there are some things I refuse to use my psychic sense to delve into, and the front of a man's pants is one of them.

## Words of Wisdom

"You don't love someone for their looks,
or their clothes, or for their fancy car,
but because they sing a song only you can hear."
~Author unknown

## USING THE PSYCHIC EDGE

Before you can find that special someone, you need to be clear about what you're looking for in your ideal man. That might be harder than it sounds. To guide you, try this exercise.

Sit in a comfortable chair in a quiet room. Close your eyes and breathe deeply three times. On each exhale, let the tension flow out of your body. Then repeat the three breaths, only this time, count out loud from one to three. You don't have to speak loudly; just a whisper will do. But it's important to hear your own voice. Concentrate on breathing and listening.

When you feel fully relaxed, begin to form a picture in your mind of your ideal man. Be as detailed as possible, including appearance, personality, profession, and anything else that's important to you. You can give him a name if one comes to you, or you can use a term of endearment, like "Darling." Sit quietly, simply visualizing him, then say out loud, "I will know you when I meet you."

This activity can be done anytime during the day when you have a spare moment, but it should definitely be done right before bed so your mind will be focused on your ideal man throughout your sleep hours. It will open up your psychic awareness to the kind of man you want and help you intuitively recognize him when you meet him. This is a very powerful tool to develop your psychic edge and find Mr. Right.

CHAPTER 2

# Why Hasn't He Called?

This is one of my clients' most frequently asked questions. Sometimes a woman will wonder about a guy she just met who took her number but never used it. Other times a woman is in a relationship with a man whom she believes is her soulmate, until one day he goes AWOL. Either way, the tears, anger, and frustration that come with waiting by the phone and perpetually checking e-mails can shake the ego of even the most confident woman.

This chapter focuses specifically on the problem of what to do when a woman thinks she's met the man of her dreams and gives him her number. She expects to hear from him right away, but he doesn't call. So she waits and waits, and gets more and more upset. What did she do to turn him off? How could she have been so wrong about him? Why does this always happen? As I've seen over the years, there are many ways the love train can be derailed before it even leaves the station.

## AMANDA AND MICHAEL

Amanda called me late one night when she was unable to sleep. She told me she had been waiting for a man named Michael to call her for more than two weeks.

"When I met Michael at a club, I just felt this instant connection with him. We spent hours dancing and talking and having a terrific time. I gave him my number, and he promised to call, but he hasn't. I can't sleep thinking about this." As Amanda told me the story of her encounter with Michael, her voice alternated between exasperation and bewilderment. She obviously assumed that Michael's failure to call was flat-out rejection, but I didn't agree.

"Have you been back to that club since you met Michael?" I asked her.

"No, I didn't want to run into him since he hasn't called me. I don't want him to think I'm desperate, and I'm definitely not going to chase him."

"Amanda, I have good news. I'm glad that you're not willing to give up your dignity for this guy, but I feel that he lost your phone number and that's why he hasn't called. If you go back to the club tonight, he'll be there and you won't seem desperate to him. It will just look like you're out having a good time with your friends." Then I added, "Believe me, he'll be happy to see you, because he's upset about not being able to get in touch with you."

It took a little convincing, but Amanda eventually agreed to return to the club.

A few days later, Amanda called me. She was very excited and couldn't wait to tell me what had happened. "He was there, just like you said!" she cried. "He came right up to me and said he'd lost my number when he dropped his cell phone in the street. He'd been going to the club ever since, hoping he would see me again. We're going out Friday night! And this time he gave me his number, too, in case his cell phone gets run over by a taxi again and he loses all his contacts."

## Lessons Learned

There are many reasons why a man might not call after you give him your number. In Amanda's case, it really was a simple case of technical difficulties. She had almost let a guy she really liked slip through her fingers because she was afraid of looking foolish. Now, I never tell women to go chasing after guys who've shown no interest in them, but this isn't one of those cases. Since Amanda had gone to the club many times before she met Michael, there was no reason to think that going there after she met him would seem "desperate." If anything, the fact that she was going out of her way to avoid the club made it seem like she'd been overly affected by his failure to call.

Instead of just writing Michael off, Amanda should have paid closer attention to her gut feelings. She felt they had really hit it off when they met, and she couldn't imagine what had happened to change that. If she had listened to her intuition, she would not have wasted time agonizing and losing sleep. Instead, she would have looked at the situation logically and realized that there was no reason she couldn't go back to the club. If she'd done that, she would have saved herself a lot of anxiety, and she could have hooked up with her guy that much sooner.

Of course, that's not a license to start stalking a guy who doesn't call after meeting you. If your gut feeling is that the man you met might actually have trouble contacting you for some reason, then it's perfectly fine to call or e-mail him once—and only once. Alternatively, if you met him during the course of your daily routine, like at your favorite coffee shop or club, it's fine to continue your usual routine where you might run into him. But calling him hourly or camping out at the coffee shop is not acceptable. By calling him once, you'll give him the tools to find you. Then the ball is in his court.

## SHIREEN AND BRIAN

A female co-worker had set Shireen up on a blind date with her cousin, Brian. Shireen called me after the date to talk it over. She had really liked Brian; he was the nicest guy she had been out with in a long time.

"When we were together, Brian was great," she said. "He picked me up and brought me flowers. Everything was wonderful. He was even sympathetic when I told him all about my old boyfriend whom I like to call 'The Jerk.'"

"It sounds like a perfect night. But I can tell there's a great big 'but' looming here. What happened?" I said.

"I think Brian might be 'The Jerk #2'! He said he wanted to go out with me again, but he never called. What's that all about?" Shireen sounded angry, but she was also clearly hurt by Brian's lack of interest in pursuing a relationship with her.

After turning over a couple of Tarot cards, I was hit by a strong feeling that something had gone wrong on the date.

I said, "You spent some of the evening telling Brian about The Jerk, right? How long did you talk about your ex?"

Shireen paused, thinking. "Um, I don't know. We talked about a whole bunch of things. I suppose a lot of them did come back to The Jerk. I was with him for a long time, so I can barely go ten minutes without seeing something that reminds me of him."

"Okay, I think we've figured out the problem," I said. "All the talk about your old boyfriend was a turn-off for Brian.

No man wants to buy a woman dinner so she can vent about her ex."

"Oh no, that couldn't be it!" Shireen cried. "I didn't talk about The Jerk that much. Besides, Brian seemed to be fine with it. He never told me to stop."

"Brian's polite. He's not going to tell you what you can talk about. I'm sorry, but I don't think he's going to call you."

Shireen sighed deeply. "Well, if he can't stand the truth about my past relationships, that's just too bad for him. But are you sure this was really the problem?" Not surprisingly, she didn't want to admit that she'd been responsible for ruining her chances with a nice guy.

"I'll tell you what," I began. "It would probably help you to have some closure with this. Why don't you ask your co-worker about Brian? He's her cousin. I feel she knows the truth and will tell you."

The next time Shireen called me, she told me what her co-worker had revealed to her. Brian thought that Shireen was pretty and seemed nice, but all the talk about her ex-boyfriend had bothered him. It made him think that she wasn't truly over The Jerk, and Brian didn't want to get involved with someone who was still hung up on another guy.

## LESSONS LEARNED

After Shireen got confirmation from her friend about why Brian hadn't called, she told me about something she remembered from their one date. She said that about halfway through the evening, she got the impression that the atmosphere had changed. She described a "funny feeling" in her stomach that she didn't understand. In hindsight, she realized that it started at about the time when she began explaining to

Brian why "The Jerk" was such an appropriate name for her ex-boyfriend.

I explained to her that the feeling she had experienced was her own psychic sense trying to tell her something. In this case, it was warning her against going on about The Jerk because it was making Brian uncomfortable. Shireen immediately understood how valuable it would be to pay attention to that sense and recognize the "funny feeling" when it happens again. And, just to be on the safe side, I also warned her to avoid talking about her ex-boyfriends to any new men she meets.

## Words of Wisdom

"Yesterday is gone. Tomorrow has not yet come.
We have only today. Let us begin."
—*Mother Teresa*

## JUST THE FACTS

What do we mean when we say someone's on the rebound? Generally we're referring to a person who's still healing from the end of a previous relationship when he or she gets involved with someone new. Conventional wisdom says that rebound relationships are doomed because a person must heal the heartache from the previous relationship before being able to fully commit to creating a healthy new one. My client Shireen is a good example of a woman who was on the rebound but didn't even know it. She wanted a new relationship, but she was still so emotionally involved with her ex that she couldn't give a new guy the attention he deserved.

So how do you avoid Shireen's mistake and know when you're ready for a new relationship? There are no hard and fast rules on the subject because every person and every break-up is different. Generally, your heart will heal faster following a two-month fling than a ten-year marriage—or not, depending on how attached you were to your partner in the previous relationship. Some people insist that it will take half as long as the relationship lasted before you're over it. That's bad news for someone whose relationship lasted twenty years because they're staring down the barrel of ten years of heartache. Fortunately, there's some help out there for women who want to know if they're really over their previous partner before diving in headfirst with someone new.

Psychotherapist Mary Darling Montero, contributor to the website BounceBack.com, offers tips to readers who want to know whether the time is right for them to get involved in a new relationship. One problem she warns against is becoming a "chronic rebounder," which is a person who frequently hops from one relationship directly into the next. Chronic rebounders might not really be in love with their new partners, but instead are simply afraid of being alone. A question she suggests you ask yourself about a possible rebound relationship is whether you went out searching for it. If you actively start searching for another boyfriend the minute the door slams on your old one, then you might just be trying to avoid working through the pain of the break-up by having a new, exciting person in your life.

Obviously, if you start a relationship for any reason besides attraction to the other person, it's a recipe for disaster. Remember, *you* are the best person to know what's right for you, as long as you know how to ask the question correctly. So if you're wondering, "Am I on the rebound?" maybe you should also ask yourself, "What does my intuition say?"

## CAROL AND WAYNE

As soon as I picked up the phone, Carol launched into her story about meeting Wayne. "My God, he was handsome! He was dressed like a pirate!"

She had met Wayne while he was walking on stilts at a street festival that she had attended with some friends. He had been hired as one of the festival's entertainers, along with some jugglers, magicians, and mimes. Wayne was a lawyer during the week, but his real passion was stilt walking on weekends.

"What a body! His shirt was open all the way down to the waist. He's perfect!" Carol gushed. Then she paused and said jokingly, "I just don't know how tall he really is."

I chuckled as I laid my Tarot cards on the table. "Okay, so what happened with him?"

"He asked me for my number, but he hasn't called yet," Carol said.

I frowned at my cards. I had an odd feeling about this guy. "Did he tell you what law firm he's with?" I asked her.

"Oh, yeah. I remembered because one of the partners there handled my sister's divorce. He did a good job, too. She got the Volvo and the summer house."

"Well, I think you should call Wayne," I said. "Tell him you were thinking about him."

"I had thought about doing that, but I don't want to seem too pushy. Do you really think I should?" Carol was hesitating, but I knew she wanted to call him.

After a little gentle prodding on my part, Carol agreed to call Wayne at work the next day. Then she called me the very next night to tell me all about it.

"First of all, thank you for telling me to call him," she said. "I don't think I would have had the guts if you hadn't told me it was all right."

"I'm glad I could help. So you got to talk to him, then?"

"Absolutely. The secretary put me right through to Wayne's office. He was excited to hear from me and told me he had planned on calling."

"Okay, that sounds promising," I said slowly. That strange feeling I'd had the day before when Carol told me about Wayne was still floating around.

"I thought it sounded promising, too, at first. Then he dropped the bombshell. He said he wanted to come over to my apartment and give me a private, naked dance show. I didn't know what to say, so he just kept talking. He said the only night he was available to come over was Wednesday, because that was his only night away from the wife and *three* kids!"

I nearly choked on my cup of tea. I had known there was something wrong with Wayne, but I didn't expect it to be this wrong. "That's horrible!" I said when I cleared my throat.

"You bet it is," Carol said. "I called him a loser and told him I never wanted to hear from him again. Then I hung up."

"You don't need me to tell you, but you were absolutely right to dump the stilt man," I assured her.

Carol blew out a disgusted breath and said, "Can you believe it? Just because a guy likes to put on a costume and walk around festivals on stilts, why does he have to be a freak?"

## LESSONS LEARNED

Carol was happy that she had called Wayne and found out what kind of guy he was. She hadn't felt a very strong connection with him, but she had thought he was good-looking. Even though he turned out to be far from what she was looking for, she told me that she was glad she'd taken matters into her own hands and called him. Otherwise she would have been sitting next to the phone wondering what had happened to him and thinking that yet another great guy had slipped through her fingers. After finding out what he was really like, she was able to let him go without a second thought. The one thing she still wondered about, though, was how tall he was.

### Words of Wisdom

"Tis easy to see, hard to foresee."
~*Benjamin Franklin*

## USING THE PSYCHIC EDGE

Many times our intuition, or psychic sense, gives us subtle physical sensations to let us know when it's trying to get our attention. Most people ignore these feelings. But if they were more in touch with their inner voice, they could interpret these psychic nudges and have a better understanding of what path they should take. This exercise can lead your intuition to become more in tune with your body.

Take four quarters and lie flat on your back on a bed. Place one quarter on the middle of your forehead, one on each shoulder, and one on the middle of your stomach. Close your eyes and try to focus on each quarter, one at a time. The quarters are very light, and the object of this exercise is to help you become more aware of the slight pressure you feel when you are getting a "gut" feeling. As you focus on each quarter, try to really feel the sensation it gives your body.

When you have experienced the sensation of each individual quarter, then try to feel them all at once. If you practice this exercise regularly, you will improve and sharpen your psychic eye.

*Optional expert level:* Once you get good at sensing the quarters, try using something lighter, like dimes or cotton balls. The better you are at feeling changes in your body, the better you will be at detecting the subtle sensations that accompany psychic awareness.

## CHAPTER 3

# Why Do I Attract Losers?

So you might meet a lot of guys, but that doesn't help if you think they're all jerks. I talk to many women who feel like they're magnets for crazies, freaks, grifters, gigolos, addicts, and convicts. On the other hand, sometimes I get calls from men who can't understand why women aren't interested in them. One thing I've discovered over the years is that both sexes can learn a lot from hearing what the other has to say.

## JESSICA AND PATRICK

"I wish you could see Patrick!" Jessica crowed. "He's the most handsome man I've ever met. When he walks into a room, all I can do is watch him. Just the way he moves and his smile—he's perfect!"

Jessica had been going on like this for a good five minutes. She was obviously over the moon about this new man she'd been seeing. Since Jessica had been a regular caller of mine for two years, I knew how long she had waited to find Mr. Right, and I was very happy for her. There was only one thing that I didn't understand.

"It's wonderful that you're so in love. Patrick sounds like a great guy," I told her. "Now, don't get me wrong, because

I'm glad to hear from you, but why are you calling me? Usually people call when they've got a problem."

"Well, that's just the thing. I do have a problem. Now that I've finally found the right guy, I'm terrified some other woman is going to snap him up."

I frowned at my Tarot cards. Psychically I didn't feel that Patrick had to fight women off. On the contrary, I believed he was more like a female repellent.

"Jessica, I don't want to insult you, but I really don't feel that he's very attractive to most women. I don't think you have anything to worry about."

"Oh no, you're wrong," Jessica assured me. "Patrick could get anyone he wants. Women love him. That's what I'm afraid of."

I decided to try another approach. "I'm confused. The cards I'm looking at show that Patrick is a good guy, but he's not what most people would call handsome. I'm seeing a short, overweight man. I think he's disfigured somehow, maybe with a scar? Is there someone else I could be seeing here?"

"Oh no. I'd never cheat on my Patrick. He's the one and only for me."

"Hmmm," I said, pondering the cards lying on the table in front of me. "Jessica, tell me something. You met Patrick, what, three months ago?"

"That's right. At my cousin's wedding. He was one of the groomsmen."

"And when you first saw him—before the two of you actually met—what was your impression of him?"

Without thinking, Jessica blurted, "I thought, 'Who's that weird old guy?'" She paused and I could hear a sharp intake of breath on the other end of the phone. "Oh my gosh, I totally forgot about that! I was sitting next to my sister in the church and we were checking out the groomsmen standing by the altar. I actually pointed out Patrick and joked with my sister about how a homeless guy had snuck into the bridal party and wondered whether he'd found his tuxedo in a dumpster."

"But now you think he's handsome. What's different about him now?" I asked. "Did he cut his hair or lose weight or something?"

"No, he looks about the same," Jessica said slowly. "Actually his hair is longer now. But I like it. He lets me pull it out of its ponytail at night when he gets home from work. It feels silky."

"So the only thing that's changed is that you know him and have feelings for him now?"

"Yeah, I guess that's right. Like now I know how he got that scar on his forehead and why he was wearing those biker boots with his tux at the wedding. I suppose other people might not think he's handsome if they just saw him on the street."

I smiled. "Fortunately, the only thing that matters is how you feel. And believe me when I say you don't have anything to worry about from other women."

## LESSONS LEARNED

If you're wondering why all the guys you meet are losers, maybe it's because you're not looking close enough. If Jessica hadn't been at a wedding when she first saw Patrick, she never would have given him a chance. When he approached her during the reception and asked for a dance, she nearly said no, but she didn't want to seem rude in front of her cousin's new family. By the end of the dance, Patrick had made her laugh, and by the end of the night, she was looking forward to going out with him the next day.

Remember that one woman's loser is another woman's superhero. The trick is being open enough to spot that one special man for you. If you listen to your intuition, you'll be able to feel a special spiritual connection with someone when he comes along. That's when things really start popping, and suddenly the Elephant Man becomes Brad Pitt.

### Words of Wisdom

"Beauty is in the eye of the beholder."
~*Margaret Wolfe Hamilton Hungerford*

## ANGELO

"Louise, this is my first time calling a psychic, but I don't know what else to do." Angelo sounded embarrassed, which is typical of men who contact me for readings. They're not used to asking strangers for help, and it makes them squeamish.

"I'm glad you called," I replied. "Why don't you tell me what's going on with you?"

There was a short pause on the other end of the phone, as though Angelo was thinking about how to phrase his question. Then he blurted out, "I can't find a woman! I'm twenty-seven years old, I've been told I'm good-looking, and I dress well and drive a nice car, but the most I get is a couple of dates with a woman before she blows me off. Why do women hate me?"

"Don't exaggerate. It'll only make you feel worse," I cautioned. "All the women in the world don't hate you. I'm a woman and I don't hate you. Tell me about a specific woman who you think hates you."

"My ex-girlfriend. We were together for four years, then one day she showed up at my place, grabbed the clothes and stuff she had left there, and took off. She wouldn't say a word to me, and since then she won't talk to me at all. I don't know what happened."

"She left a while ago, didn't she?" I asked.

"Yeah, about six months ago."

"And since then you've tried dating other women?"

"A lot of women. I don't like to be alone. I like having someone to pamper and call and take out."

"You sound like a dream come true for many women," I told him. "But I sense there's something else going on here that you're not telling me."

"No, really, there's nothing. I treat a woman like a queen when we go out. I always pay for everything, I send flowers the day after a date, I use mouthwash so I don't have bad breath... I don't understand!"

"Okay," I began calmly, trying to keep Angelo focused, "let's go back to your ex-girlfriend. You say you dated for four years. After that much time, most people would be married or living together. Why weren't you?"

Another pause from Angelo. Now we were getting somewhere. "That was her decision. She didn't like my place, and she wouldn't let me move in with her."

I turned over a couple Tarot cards, then said, "I get the feeling your place is crowded. Do you have roommates?"

"Um, no. It's my parents' house. But I have my own apartment in the attic."

"I see. Are your parents elderly or ill so they need you there to help care for them?" I asked.

"Not really. My dad's a dentist and my mom does a lot of charity work."

"So you wanted your girlfriend to move in with your parents?"

"Well, yeah. There's no point in paying rent when there's plenty of room here. My parents are busy, so they're never around. It would be just like having our own place."

"Since you're not paying for your own place, what do you do with your paychecks? Are you saving up to buy a house of your own?" It was clear what was going on here, but I wanted Angelo to be the one to say it.

"I don't really have much saved since I don't have a job," Angelo admitted. "But my dad gives me plenty of spending money. And someday I'll inherit the house. Then we'll have our own place."

"I assume your girlfriend didn't want you moving into her place because you'd just be sitting around there all day while she was out earning rent money?"

"She said something like that, but I told her it was only temporary until I get the house."

I had to stifle a sigh at this point. "When I picture your father, I see black hair and youthful energy. Is that right?"

"He just turned fifty," Angelo replied uncertainly.

"All these other women who allegedly hate you after only one or two dates, I suppose you tell them about your living arrangements when you go out?"

"Yeah, of course. I explain why we can't go back to my place and have to go to theirs if, you know, we want to be alone."

"And telling them that usually ends the date, doesn't it?"

Silence on the other end of the line.

"Angelo, listen carefully," I said. "Women don't hate you. You have a lot to offer. But not as long as you're living off your father. Women want a man with a job and a future and ambition. I feel that your father has a long, full life ahead of him, so unless you're willing to wait more than thirty years before you have another girlfriend, you've got to get something going for yourself now. Find a job, get your own apartment, and get on with your life."

More silence on the other end of the phone.

"Angelo, are you still there?" I asked.

"Isn't there something easy I could do instead? Like get a new haircut?"

## LESSONS LEARNED

I don't know what happened with Angelo after our conversation. He didn't call me again, but I hope I got through to him. You don't need to be psychic to understand that no woman wants a relationship with an overgrown teenager or someone she has to take care of. She wants an adult and a partner. And as any woman will tell you, it might be tough to live up to her high expectations, but it's definitely worth it.

Some women find themselves consistently attracting guys who are irresponsible or dependent or addicted or any number of other things that make them undesirable. These are perfectly nice women who deserve better, and they wonder what they're doing wrong. Unfortunately, they might be attracting these guys because they're so desperate to find a man that they'll put up with all sorts of nonsense.

Remember Rosie back in chapter 1, who had been bilked out of $800 by Eddie? She was so eager to find a man that she ignored her better judgment and did things she normally would never consider. Opportunists like Eddie can pick up on desperation and need the same way a vulture smells carrion. Fortunately, self-esteem works well as a weapon against guys looking to take advantage of a vulnerable woman.

## Words of Wisdom

"Necessity never made a good bargain."
~*Benjamin Franklin*

## JUST THE FACTS

American women are facing a crisis. According to the February 19, 2011, essay "Where Have the Good Men Gone?" in *The Wall Street Journal*, women in their twenties are becoming responsible, successful adults in greater numbers than men in the same age group. Women are earning more college degrees, demonstrating greater self-confidence, and making more money. Meanwhile, men in their twenties are hanging out with their friends, playing video games, and showing no signs of wanting to settle down. This growing gulf between men and women could be part of the reason that fewer than half of Americans have ever been married by the time they reach age thirty.

The article's author, Kay S. Hymowitz, says that today's young women are far more independent and successful than in previous generations. With abundant educational and career opportunities, they don't need a man to take care of them. They can even hit the local sperm bank to help them start a family. But their strides come at the expense of men, who aren't really needed anymore. In the old days, men were necessary to support women and children. Now that that's no longer the case, men aren't sure what their role is supposed to be, so they just linger in a prolonged adolescent phase.

I personally don't agree that men are immature simply because they're lost and confused by women's success. This is an interesting phenomenon, though, and it shows that our society has progressed to where a woman no longer needs to put up with any old jerk just so she'll have someone to take care of her. If a woman can't find the right guy, she can go without until the right one comes along. There's no longer a social stigma associated with being thirty years old and unmarried. You can enjoy your life and your success on your own until the guys grow up enough to deserve you. So if you're a woman in your twenties and you want to know why you attract losers, maybe it would help to know that it's not just you. A lot of men your age act like life is one big frat party. Hopefully they'll grow out of it, but in the meantime, be grateful for your own independence and maturity.

## USING THE PSYCHIC EDGE

Just because a guy looks good doesn't mean he's the right one for you. The stories of Patrick and Angelo prove that. In order to give your psychic sense a chance to help you choose Mr. Right, and reduce the importance of your eyes, try this exercise. It will take some time if you do it right, but it's worth the investment.

Sit in a quiet room on a comfortable chair. In a notebook, start listing all the characteristics that are important to you for a man to possess. You don't have to put them in order of importance; just get them down. This list might take a while to make.

Next, list the single men you know. They might be attractive to you or hideous, but put their names down on paper.

Finally, take each man's name and write it next to all the characteristics on your list that he possesses. Be sure to write out each man's full name. That's part of the process. For instance, if three of the traits you listed are "loyalty," "a sense of humor," and "great hair," and your friend Troy has those, then you'll write his name next to each of those three characteristics.

When you're done, look over your list. Whose name appears most often as having the greatest number of characteristics you value? Have you ever considered him as a romantic partner? Do you feel differently about him now after writing his name so many times next to traits that you think are important?

## CHAPTER 4

# How Can I Get Him to Notice Me?

I can't tell you how many women call me with this question. They're crazy about some guy whom they don't know very well—or not at all—and they want to figure out how to get his attention. Of course, the ultimate goal is to get the man to share the attraction they already feel.

My response is that it's usually possible to attract a man with the right actions. Unfortunately, my clients don't always pay attention when they're told what the right actions are. As you will see in the next two stories, one woman listened, but the other didn't. And one got her happily ever after, while the other is still searching for Prince Charming.

## GRACE AND JIM

Grace had joined a health club eight months before she called me. When she called, she was agitated over a guy she had spotted at the club shortly after joining. Grace had been keeping an eye on him the whole time.

"Jim is really something," she told me. "He's so cute. I think about him all the time. Do you think he notices me?"

"Yes, definitely," I said as I laid out the Tarot cards. "Actually, I think he finds you very attractive, but I don't see too much communication there."

"No, we really don't talk, but we have started saying hello to each other when we pass in the circuit training room or in the hallways."

I could see in the cards that there was potential in this relationship, so I gave Grace some advice.

"Next time you see him, ask for his advice about something, like maybe how to adjust a piece of equipment or whether you're using the right form on a machine." I felt that Jim was the kind of guy who liked to give advice and help people. "This will start the two of you talking, and you'll have more conversations. I feel it will lead to much more later."

Grace was quiet for a moment. I had a bad feeling. Something wasn't right.

"Is there a problem with doing what I suggested?" I asked Grace.

"Well, it's just that this is all going so slowly," Grace complained. After a pause, she continued slowly, "Louise, I want you to look in your cards. I'm not going to tell you what I'm going to do, but please answer one question for me. If I take the action that I'm thinking about, will it turn out all right?"

I shuffled the cards and began pulling them off the deck. They were a complete disaster.

"No, don't do it," I warned Grace quickly. "I see that whatever it is you're planning to do, it won't turn out well."

"Okay" was the only thing she said to me before hanging up.

It was a month before I heard from Grace again. When she finally called, it was immediately apparent that she hadn't listened to me. She had been impatient to start a relationship with Jim and wanted things to happen faster than what she expected if she followed my advice. The story she told left me cringing.

"I figured that if something happened to Jim's car in the health club parking lot, then he would need a ride home," she said. "So I sat in my car and waited for him to show up. Then I watched for one of the cars parked next to his to pull out so I could take that space. I hopped out and slashed his two front tires, then waited in my car for him to come out. I figured I'd be able to offer my sympathy and help. I mean, with two tires slashed, he couldn't just slap on a spare and drive away."

Her voice faltered at this point in the story. She sounded like she was going to cry. After a loud sniffle, Grace continued her tale.

"Jim did come out about half an hour later, but so did the cops."

Apparently, someone had seen Grace slash Jim's tires and had called the police.

"My sister came in the morning to bail me out," she explained. "But it was terrible. I was so embarrassed. And they took away my shoelaces."

"Oh, Grace, I can tell how bad you feel about what happened. I told you not to do it, though." I felt sorry for this poor, misguided woman, but I was also shocked at the extent of her bad judgment.

"I know. It was my fault," she admitted. Then, after a thoughtful pause, Grace said something that really made my head spin.

"Louise, I have another question. I can't see Jim at the health club anymore because they cancelled my membership after vandalizing a car in the parking lot. But he knows my phone number since it's on all the court documents. I can't help wondering, do you think he'll call me?"

## LESSONS LEARNED

If Grace had listened to me or, better yet, to her inner psychic feeling, she never would have taken the actions she did. Jim had already noticed her at the health club, so they were moving in the right direction. And even if he had no idea she existed, it's never appropriate to commit a crime in order to get a guy's attention.

Grace knew that vandalizing Jim's car was a bad idea, which is why she refused to tell me what she had planned before she did it. But she was too impatient and wouldn't let the relationship unfold naturally. Always stop, think, feel, and listen to your inner self before taking action. It will keep you from making a blunder that could not only ruin a budding relationship but also possibly put you behind bars. Needless to say, the last time I heard from Grace, Jim still had not called her, and I'm certain that he never will.

### Words of Wisdom

"People who are sensible about love are incapable of it."
~Douglas Yates

## LEXI AND EDWARD

Lexi met Edward at a football party at a mutual friend's house one Sunday afternoon.

"He was so funny. He was a nice guy and handsome, too," she told me.

Then she went on to say that they had talked for a while at the party, but Edward had left early to go home and give his cat, Figgi, a thyroid pill.

Lexi saw Edward at a couple more football parties that season at their mutual friend's house. The problem was that Edward didn't seem to pay much attention to her.

"Louise, how can I get him to notice me?" Lexi asked me. "I can tell he's a great guy; all of his friends love him. The thing is that when he's not watching the game, he talks to a couple of other cat owners about Figgi and doesn't pay any attention to me."

"Lexi," I said, laying out the cards for her, "I see that you don't initiate conversations with him. It seems like you're waiting for him to talk to you."

"That's right. I usually wait for the guy to make the first move."

"Well, Edward isn't going to do that. He's kind of shy that way. So you'll have to take the initiative if you want this to happen. I see that he loves his cat very much and is extremely concerned about Figgi's health. Ask him about his cat."

"But I don't care about cats," she said.

"You like animals, don't you?" I asked.

"Yes, but I've never had a cat."

"Well, think of this as a learning experience. Ask him about Figgi."

Lexi not only took my advice and approached Edward to talk about his cat, but also went a step further. She was walking past a pet store one day and had a psychic feeling. Listening to it, she went inside and bought a catnip mouse for Figgi. She gave it to Edward the next time she saw him. Edward loved it and launched into stories about Figgi, even asking Lexi to come over to meet his feline friend. Lexi learned that Figgi had been Edward's mother's pet before the woman passed away. Since he had promised his mother he would take good care of the cat, Edward was especially worried about the animal's developing health problems.

That catnip mouse was the beginning of everything. Lexi, Edward, Figgi, and two newly adopted kittens are all living happily ever after in a new home they bought for their expanding family.

## Lessons Learned

Sometimes the way to get a man to notice you can be a very small action. In Lexi's case, that action was stepping into a pet store. The important thing to remember is to follow your inner feelings the way Lexi did. Often, a seemingly tiny step can net big results.

### Words of Wisdom

"Can there be a love which does not make demands on its object?"

~Confucius

## Just the Facts

It's fun to watch nature programs on TV and see how animals attract mates. For instance, peacocks display the vibrant plumage of their tails to attract peahens. Male deer grow impressive racks of antlers to give them an advantage when competing with other bucks. And female olive baboons develop swollen, red bottoms a week or so before they are fertile. Research shows that the bigger a female baboon's butt grows, the more popular she becomes with male baboons. She enjoys more males competing for her attention and grooming her.

But are the criteria used in the animal kingdom really much different from the ways humans select their mates? Women might be attracted to a man with a nice car, or men might like a woman with large breasts. Are those really so different from huge antlers or a red bottom?

There's even some research to suggest that humans decide whether to have sex based as much on their own physical characteristics as those of their would-be partners. According to the study "Dating Profile Attributes vs. First Date Outcomes" by the British dating site FreeDating.co.UK, women who are either overweight or tall are more likely to have sex on a first date than smaller women. These results were based on surveys of 10,000 members of the dating site.

The researchers identified some other characteristics, in addition to physical size, that helped predict whether a woman would have sex on a first date. Those who drank alcohol, had a low level of education, and were interested in cars were more likely to engage in sexual activity after only one date. On the other hand, nondrinkers and those who rode bicycles were unlikely to engage in sex on a first date.

As for men, those who described themselves as "athletic" were more likely to have sex on a first date, as were married men who were seeking women on the online dating site. Both men and women became increasingly less likely to jump into bed as they got older.

This research suggests that you can do everything right to attract your perfect mate—have the largest breasts, or the most expensive car, or the biggest, reddest bottom on the block—but you still might not be successful because of the characteristics of the person you're after. The person simply might not be interested in what you've got to offer, and that's nothing for you to be ashamed of. Your efforts could be as futile as those of an athletic, married man who's got his eye on a short, skinny teetotaler on a bicycle.

### Words of Wisdom

"You, yourself, as much as anybody in the entire universe, deserve your love and affection."
~Buddha

## USING THE PSYCHIC EDGE

Not sure which path to take because you can't figure out what your psychic intuition is telling you? Try letting your subconscious mind tackle the problem while you get a little rest.

Some of the psychic edge exercises offered in this book, especially the ones that have to do with visualization, can be done at bedtime. This is a very powerful time to do these, as our minds are particularly open to psychic sensations as we prepare for sleep. Many of us have had psychic premonitions in our dream state. When we enter into the metaphorical "arms of Morpheus" (the Greek god of dreams), our psychic eye is at its most sensitive.

Take a nice warm shower. This will help you unwind. Lie down comfortably in bed and take a few minutes to look up at the ceiling. Say quietly, "I will see in my dreams the right man for me." Repeat this statement three times. Now close your eyes and relax. Repeat the statement three more times before you fall asleep.

You'll be surprised by the dreams you have once you begin using this exercise. Everyone is different, so some people will see results quickly, while others will have to wait longer. Either way, keep up the practice regularly and results will eventually come to you.

I assigned this exercise to a client of mine named Mary Jo. She started doing it every night. After a month she had her first dream about a rather short, average-looking man with a joyful smile and laughing blue eyes. The dreams continued at a rate of two or three times a week for several months. Then one morning Mary Jo stopped for coffee, and standing in line next to her was the man she had been dreaming about.

She immediately knew this was an important moment in her life, and Mary Jo did something she normally never did: she started talking to the stranger. His name was Ted, and they ended up having coffee together, then exchanged numbers and started dating. Ted told her later that he was instantly attracted to her, but he thought she was too pretty for him, and he never would have talked to her first.

This exercise was an important tool in opening up Mary Jo's dream state to the psychic realm, and it can work for you, too.

## CHAPTER 5

# What's He Doing with That Other Woman?

We all accumulate baggage as we go through life, and this includes a variety of past and current relationships. Unfortunately, it's hard for some women to accept this fact about the men they're interested in. A common complaint I hear from my clients is that the guy they're dating has another woman in his life. She might be a remnant from his past who has popped up again, or she could be someone new who is competing for his attention. The circumstances vary, but the central problem remains: there's another woman in the picture.

My clients feel a great deal of anxiety, jealousy, competition, and heartache over "the other woman." Countless women have told me that they can't sleep or eat because they're so busy obsessing over what he's doing with "her." The stress inevitably causes their relationship with the guy to suffer, which only makes them more miserable. It's a downward spiral that's to be avoided if you're in search of a successful, happy, healthy relationship.

# KIMBERLY AND CHRIS

Kimberly called me one day to ask about her boyfriend, Chris. They had met on a social networking site.

"It was love at first sight. He's so hot!" Kimberly told me, her voice cooing softly into the phone.

I had a feeling that Chris was indeed hot, but Kimberly wasn't the only woman who thought so.

"Yes, Kimberly, I feel you and Chris have a very special connection." As I talked, I shuffled my Tarot deck.

"You're right!" Kimberly exclaimed. "It's so special between us. I've never felt this way about a guy in my life."

"But there's a problem," I said. Studying the cards in front of me, I knew there was a blond woman in the picture.

"I was looking at his profile page a few weeks ago, and his ex-girlfriend, Maria, has started posting there. When I mentioned it to him, he said they're just friends and that I shouldn't be jealous. But I know there's more going on than he's telling me." Kimberly drew in a ragged breath, and I could hear that she was close to tears.

I gave her a moment to collect herself and then said, "You've been doing something secretive, haven't you?"

On the other end of the phone, Kimberly gasped. She knew she'd been caught red-handed. After some weak denials, she finally came clean with me.

"I've been able to sneak in and read Maria's profile page without being on her list of friends. She's posting lyrics for all kinds of love songs and bragging about going out with her ex. She said it's only a matter of time before they're back together." Kimberly was sobbing now.

"Why is Chris even talking to her?" she cried. "Does he think she's better than me?"

I tried to comfort Kimberly as I spread more Tarot cards on the table. I could see in the cards that Chris not only was talking to his old girlfriend, but he'd also seen her a couple times. For her part, Maria was hot on his trail, as relentless as a bloodhound. I also saw that Kimberly's relationship with Chris wasn't solid enough yet for her to make demands on him. They hadn't been together for very long, and he had more of a past with Maria. I explained all of this to Kimberly.

"Well, what should I do?" she asked, blowing her nose. "I know I'm going to lose him. We had a big fight the other day when I accused him of sleeping with her."

"You won't lose him if you follow my advice. It might be difficult, but this is what you need to do."

"All right," Kimberly said, sounding leery.

"Chris's ex is acting as sweet as possible to get him to pay attention to her because she wants him back. Things between them had never been great, which is why they broke up. Also, Maria is exaggerating on her profile page. You should stop eavesdropping on it because it will only drive you crazy." I paused to let that sink in before giving Kimberly her toughest assignment.

"And most important, you should never mention Maria's name to Chris again. Don't nag him about her. Just be yourself and forget about the ex. Your job is to concentrate on enjoying your time with Chris. If you're having fun, he'll have fun, and you'll both be happy."

"But what if she—"

"No buts!" I cut in. "Not a word about Maria. Just enjoy your time with Chris."

Kimberly reluctantly agreed.

Three months passed, then one day I picked up the phone to hear Kimberly's cheerful voice on the other end.

"Louise, I had to call you. Chris and I are engaged! We're getting married next June!" She sounded nothing like the sobbing girl I had talked to a few months earlier.

"That's fantastic, Kimberly! Tell me what happened."

She said she had taken my advice and stopped bugging Chris about Maria. Instead, they enjoyed themselves when they were together, and their relationship grew stronger.

"What about Maria?" I asked.

Kimberly laughed. "She didn't take your advice, and boy, did it cost her!"

Apparently, Maria had started making demands on Chris, nagging him to come to her house, take her out for dinner, and call her multiple times a day. She started acting jealous about his relationship with Kimberly, too. Maria originally claimed that she had gotten back in touch with Chris for "friendship," but then she had turned into a borderline stalker who wanted to know where he was every minute of the day.

The end came when Chris explained to Maria that he didn't want to start up his relationship with her again, and they were better off just being friends. In a rage, Maria stormed home and flew to her computer. She posted a comment on her profile page that said, "My ex-boyfriend's penis smells like bleu cheese!"

## LESSONS LEARNED

Too often, women focus on the threat of other women rather than making their relationship with their guy the best it can be. Both men and women gravitate to people who make them feel good. They don't want to be around someone who makes them miserable with whining or jealousy or nagging. Make the time you spend with the object of your desire the best it can be, and you'll see that he wants to spend more time with you.

## VERONICA AND ALAN

I remember the first time I talked to Veronica. She was very excited about this great guy she had met through a group of old college friends. His name was Alan, and according to Veronica, they had clicked immediately.

"The moment I looked into his eyes, I knew he was 'the one.' I'm sure he felt the same way," she told me at the time, and she stuck to her guns for well over a year. Meanwhile, I had my own feelings about their relationship.

"Louise, I know he loves me. You agree, don't you?" she asked me one day.

I looked in my cards, and I could see that Alan did care for her, but the cards had always shown that he wanted to continue to play the field. Something was missing for him, and I had warned Veronica many times about what I saw.

"Yes, the cards show Alan has deep feelings for you, but nothing has changed. He's still not sure," I said.

There was a long pause on Veronica's end of the line. When she began to speak again, it was in a quieter, less upbeat tone.

"I got real pissed at him the other night," she admitted. "Alan told me he couldn't see me Saturday because he was going out with someone else, but he could see me Sunday. I told him that it's been fifteen months, and it's about time we were exclusive." Veronica was agitated, and I could hear the anger in her voice. "All these bimbos are always calling him. I told him it had to stop."

"Hmmm...what did he say?" I asked as I laid down more cards.

The cards said the same things to me that they'd been saying for the past year: Alan wanted his freedom, he wasn't ready to settle down, and he wasn't nearly as sure of his feelings for Veronica as she was about her feelings for him. I could feel psychically that the balance was off in their relationship.

"He told me he could do whatever he wanted," Veronica said. "I know he's afraid to lose me, so I told him not to call me again unless he's willing to be exclusive. I could tell he was afraid. Louise, don't you think he was afraid?" she asked. Veronica wanted to sound confident, but the very fact that she was asking me to back up what she felt proved that she had serious doubts.

"Well, I'm not exactly sure he's afraid," I began carefully, "but I know he'd like to hear from you."

"No way am I calling him. He's going to have to chase me," she said smugly.

"In that case, I wouldn't expect contact from him any time soon," I warned her. The Tarot cards on my table showed no contact from him at all.

Over the course of the next month, I received many calls from Veronica as she vented her frustration at Alan's silence. Then one night, she called me in tears. She said that she finally couldn't stand it anymore and had taken matters into her own hands.

"I just decided to go over to his house, march up to the door, and ask him if he had made up his mind about me." Veronica's tears suddenly stopped and her voice turned angry. "When he answered the door, he wouldn't let me in because his 'girlfriend' was over. He told me, right in the doorway, that he had finally found the woman he had been looking for all his life! When I asked him 'What about us?' he said there had never been any 'us.' Then he closed the door in my face and left me standing on the porch. Louise, why didn't I see this coming?"

## LESSONS LEARNED

Veronica had tried so hard to make things work with a guy who just didn't feel the same way about her. There were plenty of signs that things weren't going to work out, including my warnings about what I saw in the cards and Alan's own words and actions. Plus, if she had taken the time to listen, Veronica would have heard the same message from her own psychic intuition. There's obviously a problem when the two partners in a relationship want vastly different things. If she had paid attention to the signs, Veronica wouldn't have wasted so much precious time on Alan.

After she finally let Alan go, Veronica asked me if there was something she could have done to change how he felt about her. It was like she thought there must have been something wrong with her that she could have fixed. The fact is that there are many reasons why men might not want to be exclusive. In Alan's case, he just didn't feel "it" for her. Whatever the reason a man wants to continue to play the field, a woman has a powerful advantage if she understands exactly where she stands with him. It's pointless to deny the facts and walk around with blinders on. If you don't want to be part of some man's stable of honeys, then accept the situation and go find a man who will give you what you want.

As for Veronica, it was a full year before she found herself in a new relationship where they mutually felt "it" for each other. She didn't have to give him ultimatums or feel threatened by other women. Her new guy was thrilled to have Veronica in his life. And in the end, she was happy it didn't work out with Alan. Last time she heard, he had gone through three new girlfriends and was still looking for Ms. Right.

## JUST THE FACTS

If it seems to you that men spend more time playing the field than women do, you're absolutely right. According to a 2007 research study of 6,237 American adults conducted for the National Center for Health Statistics (part of the U.S. Centers for Disease Control and Prevention), "Drug Use and Sexual Behaviors Reported by Adults: United States, 1999–2002," men average nearly twice as many sexual partners as women during their lives, and far more men than women have over a dozen sexual partners.

Researchers learned that the average American man had sex with a median number of seven different women in his lifetime. Compare that to a median of only four partners for the average woman. The differences become even more pronounced when you look at study participants who had a large number of sexual partners. Nearly 29 percent of the men surveyed told researchers they had slept with fifteen or more women, while only 9 percent of women claimed to have been with that many men.

Is it possible that men overestimated their number of sexual partners in the survey, while women underestimated their total? Absolutely. Especially since it's unclear with whom the men are having all these relationships if the women are limiting their number of sexual partners. However, the researchers tried to deal with that problem by surveying participants anonymously using a computerized system instead of having a human researcher ask questions and record answers. They hoped to avoid giving the test subjects any reason to brag or be embarrassed, because those feelings might cause the participants to intentionally report incorrect information.

But even if there are some reporting errors in the results, the fact remains that American men seem to be having more sex with more different people than women are. That discrepancy might partly explain why some women are eager to get serious before their men are: they don't have the same desire to try different flavors of "ice cream" before settling down with their favorite. It doesn't mean that either group is right or wrong. In general, men and women simply approach relationships differently, and trying to force someone to change his or her fundamental nature is a strategy doomed to fail.

## Words of Wisdom

"Sex without love is an empty experience,
but, as empty experiences go, it's one of the best."
~Woody Allen

# USING THE PSYCHIC EDGE

You can think of your own psychic ability as a muscle. The more you use it, the stronger it gets. Conversely, if it doesn't get regular workouts, then it grows weak and might not be available when you really need it. This is an example of the old adage "Use it or lose it." Making your psychic "muscle" stronger can bring you tremendous benefits in every area of your life, particularly when you're trying to navigate your love life's turbulent waters. After all, wouldn't it be nice to know what the man you want is thinking and what actions you should take to make your relationship successful? The following exercise will flex your psychic muscles.

Sit in a comfortable chair at a table with a pair of dice. Pick up one of the dice and hold it between the palms of your hands. Close your eyes. Concentrate on the sensation of the die between the palms of your hands. Feel how hard and smooth it is, and how there are little indentations on each side where the dots are. Now, visualize the die in your hands. Visualize every curve of the die, every mark, and the contrast of the colors between the dots and the rest of the die.

When you have a strong picture in your mind, try to feel which number will come up when the die falls. Visualize the die falling and which side lands face-up on the table. Then pull your palms apart and let the die fall. See how close you were to feeling the number that appeared. Repeat the process with the other die.

Don't be frustrated if the numbers aren't correct very often. It will take time for you to improve, but you should notice steady improvement as your mind exercises your psychic ability.

## SECTION TWO
# Feeling Love

## CHAPTER 6

# Why Did He Suddenly Stop Calling?

So you've found the right guy and you're ready to start living happily ever after. But since when has the course of true love ever run smoothly? All the chapters in this section address common roadblocks that trip women up when they're blissfully gazing into their partner's eyes instead of watching the ground under their feet.

Back in section 1, I spent a chapter talking about how to handle the situation where a man takes a woman's phone number when they meet or have a first date but then he never calls. In this chapter I will take a look at a different permutation on the man's failure to call. Sometimes a couple is cruising along in what seems like a happy relationship, but suddenly the man disappears. He stops calling, texting, and e-mailing. The woman tries to contact him—repeatedly and in a variety of ways—but she gets no response. The woman feels like she's been dropped off a cliff. So she gets in touch with a psychic, desperate to know "What happened?!?"

## BARBARA AND JEFF

Barbara is a sophisticated, successful advertising executive who called me crying. She was going crazy trying to figure out when Jeff was going to contact her. They had been going out for two months, and the connection between them was, in Barbara's words, "magical." They had spent every weekend together from the time they met at a marketing conference. Jeff frequently surprised her with little gifts and called at least twice a day when they weren't together.

"He was my hairy Jewish prince, my soulmate," Barbara lamented between sobs.

Everything had been going fine, she said, until one day he suddenly stopped calling. Barbara called and e-mailed him repeatedly, but he never answered. His last contact had been three weeks earlier.

Since then, this once self-assured woman had become a nervous wreck. Thoughts of Jeff interfered with every aspect of her life. She could barely sleep or eat. Every night she'd lie awake in bed clutching her cell phone, ready to answer his call. But it never came.

As I listened to Barbara, I laid out my Tarot cards and took a quick glance in my crystal ball. I could feel there was fear in Jeff.

"Barbara," I began, "first of all, please stop the drama. It won't work with this guy. All you're doing is driving him further away from you. That shows clearly in the cards."

There was one last sniffle on the other end of the phone. Then Barbara said quietly, "Really?"

"That's right," I said. "You said your relationship was magical, but I can see that things were going so fast that it was beginning to frighten Jeff. He's never experienced anything like this before."

"That's…that's good, right?" Barbara asked. "It sure sounds better than what I thought you'd say. But what can I do?"

I was pleased to hear that she had stopped crying and was listening carefully to what I was saying.

I advised Barbara to lighten things up with Jeff. Instead of leaving him desperate messages about needing to hear from him, I told her to send him something funny.

"Something funny? Like what?" she asked.

"Send him a short joke. Make sure you keep it short. I feel he likes jokes."

"Okay, that sounds easy. Is there anything else I can do?"

"Yes. Twice a day, look into a mirror, hold up your hands, and say three times, 'Jeff, come to me!' Sound vibration is very powerful. This will bring him to you faster. I feel the two of you should be together, so he will hear you."

Barbara called me two weeks later to report success. She had followed my advice and sent Jeff a goofy joke in a text message. She had resisted the urge to follow up the joke with her usual message of "I miss you! Please call me!" A few days later, Jeff called her. He apologized for his behavior and said he loved her. She was overjoyed to have her "prince" back.

## Lessons Learned

A man will never call if he expects to be dragged into drama. Something most men do like is a joke. That's why I frequently advise my clients to text their guys a joke if it's been a while since they've heard from him. Just a quick joke is a good way to get his attention and keep things light. The joke I usually recommend is simple:

*Question:* What do you get if you cross a penis and a potato? *Answer:* A dick-tater.

This joke has nearly a 100 percent success rate for getting a quick response from a guy. If you want a man's attention, you've got to talk about things he's interested in, like penises and food.

When Barbara turned down the heat on her desperation, she stopped pushing Jeff away. If she had only remained calm when he stopped calling and tried to get in touch with her own intuition, she would have been able to respond to him without making things worse. He was already fearful about getting involved so fast, and Barbara's desperate attempts at communication just pushed him further away.

Barbara told me later that Jeff had opened up to her about his feelings once they got back together. He had a history of bad experiences in the romance department, and he thought this relationship must be too good to be true. Then after all of Barbara's crazy calls, he decided he'd been right. But when Barbara sent him a playful joke, the energy shifted and he started missing her. He remembered the good times they had shared, and he found himself going to bed at night thinking about her, then waking up in the morning thinking about her some more.

Barbara still calls me on occasion, and she once confided in me that even now, when she wakes up in the morning, she whispers three times, "Jeff, come to me!" She doesn't really need to, since he's asleep next to her, but she says it keeps her focused on him and their relationship.

## Words of Wisdom

"The simple lack of her
is more to me than others' presence."
~*Edward Thomas*

# Justine and Brad

"I just don't understand why he can't make the time to talk to me. I make time to talk to him. Plus, I make time to talk to my sisters and my friends, and they make time for me. It's just what people who care about each other do, you know?"

Justine was a college sophomore who had called to tell me about her new boyfriend, Brad. I had talked to her a few times before, usually about other relationships that hadn't lasted past the first month or so. She was concerned that Brad's lack of interest in talking to her on the phone suggested that this relationship wasn't going to hit the two-month mark either.

"How often do you want to talk to him?" I asked.

"Not much. Just a few times a day. Like first thing in the morning on my way to class. You know, just to say hello, then sometimes I'll text him if I'm bored during class. Then of course during lunch, just to check in. And later when I get back to the dorm. Then we can tell each other about our day. And then later to say good night, if we're not going to see each other."

"It sounds like you want to talk to him an awful lot. What do you say to each other all the time?" Frankly, I make my living talking on the phone, but I still can't imagine wanting to talk to any one person that much.

"You know, we just talk about the usual. 'How was your day?' 'How did you do on your test?' 'What are you doing tonight?' That kind of stuff."

"Okay, so what exactly is the problem?" I asked, even though I had a pretty good idea.

"Well, when we first got together, he'd always return my calls right away. Even if he was in class, he'd send me a text to let me know he was busy, then he'd call afterward. But now he almost never answers when I call, and he doesn't reply to my texts at all. I don't know what to do, since this is how it started before my last few boyfriends dumped me."

"They dumped you?" I asked. "What did they say?"

"That's just it—they didn't say anything. They just stopped calling. No matter what I did, they wouldn't answer my calls. Finally, I even went over to their apartments, but their roommates said they weren't home, even though I knew they were. I don't want that to happen with Brad, too, but I don't know what to do!"

I took a deep breath. This wasn't going to be easy, but I had to make sure Justine understood what I was saying or she'd keep messing up her relationships.

"What you need to do is back off," I told her in a clear voice.

"What?" She was obviously surprised by my bluntness.

"You're smothering these guys with your constant calls and texts and demands for attention. Most men don't like to talk on the phone as much as women do, but you're treating these boyfriends of yours like they're no different from your sisters and friends. But they are different. They're guys. And you need to recognize that if you're going to have a successful relationship with them."

"But why wouldn't they want to talk to me? If you care about someone, that's what you do."

"You've said that twice now," I pointed out, "but remember there are different ways of showing how much you care. I feel that the guys you're attracted to tend to be athletic, right?" I could see from the Tarot cards in front of me that

Justine preferred a certain type, and you wouldn't find any of them in the college chess club.

"Yeah, Brad's on the basketball team, and the guy before him was into karate."

"And they're not big talkers when you're together, right? They let you dominate the conversation?"

"Well, yeah, I guess I talk a lot. But they seem to like it. They say I'm funny."

"And you are," I assured her. "However, they just don't enjoy talking as much as you do. What happened with the karate man and the guy before him and the guy before him was that you wanted to spend so much time on the phone that they couldn't satisfy you. If you really like Brad, you need to recognize his needs and back off a little."

"So I'm not supposed to call him? Then what if he doesn't call me? I might never see him again."

"That's a risk you're going to have to take," I acknowledged. "However, I feel that you haven't driven him so far away yet that the relationship can't be saved. You're close, though. If you keep going the same way, he's going to be history before you know it."

When I talked to Justine a month later, she was as happy as a clam—although she was especially chatty.

She told me, "Brad and I are still together! I did what you said and started calling him only once a day. It took a few days, but he finally called me. We had a nice conversation—I kept it short like you said. Then later I texted him a short joke the way you said I should. Everything's going great! Thanks so much for your advice!"

"You're welcome, Justine. I'm glad it's all working out. But how are you doing without having Brad to talk to as much as you'd like?"

"Just fine. I'm talking to one of my sisters more now, and at a family dinner a couple weeks ago, her husband thanked me for keeping her busy so he can get more work done at the office. I guess it's working out for everyone!"

## LESSONS LEARNED

It might be politically incorrect to say so, but men and women are different. They need different things in life, and to ignore that fact is a surefire way to doom a relationship. Plus, it's important to realize that there's no way you can get everything you need from one person. That's why it's important to have a network of family and friends and colleagues who can help you exercise the many aspects of your personality.

If someone offered you two free tickets to a ballet, whom would you bring with you? Now what if someone offered you two tickets to a football game? Would you bring the same person? Probably not. And how about tickets to a designer fashion show? Or a charity ball? Different people in our lives fill different roles. Your new love interest can't be all things to you any more than you can expect to be everything to him. Which is good, because it might save you from being the person who has to keep him company at a monster truck rally some day.

### Words of Wisdom

"Fear less, hope more, eat less, chew more, whine less,
breathe more, talk less, say more, love more,
and all good things will be yours."
~Swedish proverb

## Just the Facts

There are conflicting viewpoints out there over whether women actually talk more than men do. The stereotype of the chatty wife and her long-suffering, silent husband has been around for decades, but is it accurate? In her 2006 book *The Female Brain*, psychiatrist Louann Brizendine reported that women talk a lot more than men, with the average woman saying 20,000 words a day compared to only about 7,000 for the average man. However, that study was called into question the following year when new research reported that men and women both say about 16,000 words per day.

Whether men actually say fewer words than women or not, they might simply be less interested in communication. According to Dr. Brizendine, men's brains aren't set up for the same level of verbal acrobatics that women's are. Dr. Brizendine says that testosterone actually limits development in the portions of the brain devoted to communication. This starts even before birth, and it includes not only speech but also a male's ability to listen.

What this research suggests is that when you're trying to drag your man into a discussion about anything from the movie you just saw to where your relationship is headed, it's like you're trying to box with someone who's got one hand tied behind his back. Is it any wonder he doesn't want to play?

## Using the Psychic Edge

If you want to draw someone to you, try this technique that worked for Barbara in the story at the beginning of this chapter.

First thing in the morning, look in a mirror. Hold your hands palms up as though someone is handing you a gift. Close your eyes and say, "[Name of person], come to me!" Repeat three times. Do this again every night before you go to bed.

When you're doing this, try to clear your mind of all thoughts except the words you're saying. Concentrate on each word. There are only four little words, but say them slowly. Linger on the name for a moment. Visualize writing the name of the person you want. Breathe in and out slowly while you focus. Push all thoughts of sadness or longing for this person out of your mind. Practice makes perfect. The longer you do this, the better at it you will get—and the sooner you will receive the object of your desire.

This technique works because sound vibrations are very powerful in the psychic realm. As you say the name of your beloved, not only does it send the sound vibration out into the universe but it also causes you to focus. The focus clears your mind and opens up the psychic realm to you. It helps you understand your beloved, which allows you to take the appropriate actions and make the right decisions to bring him to you.

This same technique can work for anything you want, like a new job or a car. Instead of saying "[Name of person], come to me!," you can try "Legal assistant job, come to me!" or "Little red convertible, come to me!" Remember to stay focused and visualize what you desire.

CHAPTER 7

# Is He "The One"?

When we think about how it will feel when Mr. Right finally comes along, we anticipate the joy and excitement of finally finding our destiny. When we see our friends finding love and settling down, the sense of what we're missing becomes even keener and we redouble our efforts to find the man of our dreams. The problem starts when a woman is so eager to find him that she forces herself to see something in a man that just isn't there. It's natural to want to find the right person, but too many women mistakenly convince themselves that they've found their prince when they're actually just kissing another in a long line of frogs.

## JOANNE AND ROB

Much as I hate to admit it, I found Joanne to be a very frustrating client. She called me often to talk but rarely considered any advice I gave her. Like clockwork once a month, Joanne would call me with stories about the new man she had met. To her, every man was a "dreamboat," or a "soulmate," or "my ticket out of Dodge."

I never had a good feeling about any of the men she called me about, but she never listened to me. In all cases, she spent a lot of money she didn't have on new clothes, homemade gourmet dinners, and little presents for him, only to be disappointed a short time later when the guy dumped her. Then when her huge credit card bill showed up, she'd slip into a depressed funk.

One day she called me to see what I thought about a guy named Rob.

"Oh my God, Louise! He's 'the one'! I know it. I just know it," Joanne gushed.

"I don't know, Joanne. I don't get a good feeling about him, but let me shuffle my cards and see what they say."

As I shuffled my Tarot cards, Joanne started laughing.

"Louise, you may have been right about my men before, but I think you're going to be wrong this time. See, I used to date this guy back in high school, and he just found me on the Internet. He became a college professor and moved to Florida."

"Really? So you know him from your past?" I asked. Despite my misgivings, I had to admit that this relationship was showing a little more promise than Joanne's earlier ones. I've found that there's often an advantage to knowing someone's family and background. It gives the couple something in common, and they're more likely to share values.

"That's right. Rob told me he never forgot me and has always loved me. This guy is different. He's really great."

"Joanne, for your sake, I hope I'm wrong, but why do I see a woman in the cards I'm looking at? And it's a serious relationship, too. He's either engaged or married."

She hesitated, then admitted, "Well, yes. Technically he is married, but it won't be for long."

"What do you mean 'it won't be for long'?" I felt a chill shoot through my body. This was not good. It was way more than just an impending divorce.

"Rob's been married for almost twenty years, but his wife has terminal cancer and they don't expect her to live more than a few months."

I dropped my head into my hands.

"Joanne, don't you think there's something wrong with this picture?" I asked.

"It's okay! We're not doing anything with each other now while he's still married," she said quickly. "He says he wants to fly up to see me later. You know, after his wife passes. If we feel the same about each other, we can get married."

"His wife hasn't even left this earth yet and he's planning his next marriage?" I asked incredulously. I laid out layer after layer of Tarot cards on the table in front of me. All of them spelled one thing: disaster.

"Yes, but this is different. We knew each other before, and he told me he's never forgotten me."

"Listen, Joanne, the cards show that this will not work out. You shouldn't be involved with a man whose wife is lying on her deathbed. This is an emotionally unstable situation for everyone involved." I turned a few more cards, then added, "If you get married, it won't last long. I wish you would at least consider what I'm seeing here. And if you won't listen to me, please take a step back and ask yourself whether you're doing what's right."

"Okay, I will," she agreed. Right before hanging up, she added, "But I know you're wrong."

Six months passed before I heard from Joanne again. When she finally called me, a lot had happened in her life.

Rob's wife had passed away, and Rob flew up to see Joanne a week after the funeral. Joanne told me that after five glorious days together, they had decided to get married right away. Joanne got rid of all her furniture, her car, and everything else she owned with the exception of her clothes. She told me she hadn't wanted to move everything a thousand miles, plus her old things depressed her and reminded her of her old life.

"Rob was so sweet at first," she said with a little quiver in her voice. "Then he started to act strange. I felt like he was avoiding me. About a month ago he bought me a plane ticket so I could attend my cousin's wedding. I wanted him to come with, but it was during final exam week so he couldn't get away from the classes he was teaching. He drove me to the airport, kissed me goodbye, and that was the last time I ever saw him."

"What happened?" I asked, shuffling my cards to see what they would show.

"When I flew back a week later, I took a cab home, but my key wouldn't fit the lock. I could see in the windows that all the furniture was gone. There was nothing left."

"He went far away, didn't he?" I could see in the cards the great distance between them.

"Yep, he moved everything out and put the house up for sale. He got a new job at a college in California."

"You were gone for only a week. He got a lot done in a short time," I observed.

"Not exactly. His parents are dead, but my mom still has some connections to his family from the old neighborhood. She got the scoop for me. Turns out Rob started looking for a new job just a couple weeks after we got married."

"So he knew right away that it wasn't going to work out," I concluded.

"That's right. The only message he left me was through his attorney. Rob said that he wanted to be free, and I wasn't the person for him."

Joanne sniffled a little but sounded pretty upbeat, all things considered.

"The worst part is that I lost everything when I moved," she said. "Now I have to start all over again. What a bastard."

"If it helps, I can see in the cards that you're going to be fine. You're better off without him."

"You're probably right." Joanne paused, then said hopefully, "You know, just last week, I met this guy named Pete at the coffee shop. I'm sure you're going to tell me he's a great guy."

## LESSONS LEARNED

In her impatience to find "the one," Joanne caused one disaster after another in her life. Time after time she put herself in a hole, not only financially but also emotionally. Like so many other women in her position, if she had been patient and used her intuition and common sense, she would have had the potential to find a fantastic partner. But impatience makes intuition fly out the window.

### Words of Wisdom

"A lady's imagination is very rapid; it jumps from admiration to love, from love to matrimony, in a moment."

~Jane Austen

# LIZ AND KEVIN

Liz always brought a smile to my face when she called. She was hopeful that the right man was ready to step into her life in spite of many disappointments. Her attitude was particularly admirable since it was rare for Liz to go on a third date with anyone.

"Louise, tell me what you feel," she said. "Craig and I seemed to be having a great time when we went out for dinner, but it's been two weeks and he hasn't called me."

I laid out my Tarot cards and could immediately see the problem.

"Liz, I see that Craig liked you, but he couldn't figure you out. I don't want to be rude, but to be honest he thought you were a little strange."

"Oh, that again," Liz said with an exasperated sigh.

"Yes, I'm sorry, but you might as well check him off your list," I admitted as I pulled a couple more cards off the top of my Tarot deck. "Craig won't be calling you—just like the rest."

We didn't bother discussing the underlying problem that Liz had with all her relationships: she had a passionate interest in UFOs. When she went out with men, she'd always find herself talking about the UFO she had seen one night while taking an evening walk with her dog. Liz would regale her dates with all the details of the flying, disk-shaped craft that hovered twenty feet above her, the beam of light shooting out at her, and the alien ship taking off like lightning into the sky.

This experience had, understandably, made a huge impression on Liz. After extensive research on the topic of UFOs, she considered herself an expert on the subject and wanted to share all this information with her dates. Most of her dates acted polite while she told her story, but they never called again for another date.

"Louise, do you think I should wait to tell these guys about the spaceship I saw? Maybe until we've been going out for a while? When I tell them on our first or second date, they think I'm a weirdo or something," she said in exasperation.

"No, Liz, I think you're doing the right thing by being yourself. If they don't understand, too bad. There are lots of men in the world." After studying the cards on the table for a moment, I added, "And it looks like there's good news. The cards are showing someone coming into your life within the next month. He'll be special. I think he could be 'the one.'"

"Gosh, Louise, I hope so. I'm just so tired of being alone," Liz said quietly.

It was two months before Liz called me again. She giggled and said she had been very busy with a new guy. His name was Kevin.

"Louise, you were so right! I met Kevin two weeks after we talked. He's the most interesting guy I've ever met. I think…no, I *know* he's the one I've been waiting for," she said.

"I'm laying out the cards right now and I see the marriage card here," I told Liz. "I'm so happy for you. I can see he's in it for the long run."

"You want to hear the best part?" Liz asked excitedly. "You know how the other guys all thought I was a weirdo because of my UFO experience? Well, Kevin thinks it's the coolest thing he's ever heard. He told me he's always wanted to see a flying saucer but never has, so he wanted to hear all about it. He even brought his telescope over to my house on our second date, and we sat in the yard talking, drinking wine coolers, and watching the sky. By the way, Kevin wanted me to ask you a question. If we go to Roswell for vacation, will we see a UFO or anything?"

## LESSONS LEARNED

The important thing to remember when looking for "the one" is to be yourself. There's no use pretending to be someone you aren't. You want someone to know you and love you for who you are. Many women (and men, for that matter) are "on stage" when they go on dates, keeping up an act that hides the real them. If you can't act like yourself with someone, then he isn't the one for you. Hiding who you really are can lead to an unsatisfying relationship in the long run. Even if it takes a little longer to find "the one," as in Liz's case, it will be well worth the wait.

In case you're wondering, the last I heard, Kevin still hadn't seen his first UFO, but he's still watching the skies—with Liz by his side.

### Words of Wisdom

"We come to love not by finding a perfect person, but by learning to see an imperfect person perfectly."
~Sam Keen

## JUST THE FACTS

Women want to find the man of their dreams, and a British study proved that they're putting their money where their mouths—or, in this case, hearts—are. In 2010 the British dating website UKDating.com surveyed more than two thousand of its members and found that the average woman spends the U.S. equivalent of about $3,000 on dating before finding someone she wants to settle down with.

The $3,000 figure represents the estimated cost of twenty-four dates, which is the average number of dates that survey participants went on before finding the right guy. A lot of the money was spent on preparations for the dates, like a trip to the salon, a new outfit, and transportation to or from the date. Many of the women also reported paying for at least part of the date itself, including dinner and entertainment. Some generous women even purchased small gifts for the men they were going out with.

How well did the expenditures pay off? It turns out that some women fared better than others. While the average woman went out twenty-four times before finding a man she was happy with, a lot of the women had to keep trying—and spending—for much longer. One percent of the women surveyed said they went on as many as eighty dates before finding the right guy.

This study also asked women how many dates it takes with a particular guy to figure out whether he might be what they're looking for. As anyone who's ever been on a lousy date knows, it doesn't take long. A quarter of the women surveyed said they could tell if a guy was right for them after meeting just once, and over 75 percent of women needed three or fewer dates. It's also interesting to note that one-third of the women had bailed out on a date before it was over because they knew they were wasting their time.

Considering how expensive dating is, it's a good thing that many women can size up a guy quickly. It's like being in a taxi when you realize the driver is headed the wrong way. Sometimes the best thing you can do is hop out.

## USING THE PSYCHIC EDGE

When you're trying to figure out if the new man in your life is "the one," it helps if you can call on your own psychic sense to assist you. This exercise will show you how to turn a deck of playing cards into a simple and convenient way to develop and heighten your psychic awareness. A deck of cards not only has the two distinct colors of red and black but also has four different suits. That makes this exercise more challenging than the earlier one using a pair of dice.

Take an ordinary deck of playing cards. Sit quietly in a comfortable chair at a table. Remove the ace of hearts and the king of spades from the deck. Stare at each one separately, taking in the color and detail of each card. Now turn the two cards over so they're face-down. Mix them up so you don't know which card is which. With both cards lying flat on the table six inches apart, place your right palm over one of them. Now, with your eyes closed, try to "feel" through your hand the shape and color of each card. Take your time; don't rush. Feel free to go back and forth multiple times between the two cards. Remember, the important thing about this exercise is to try to "feel" it. Don't turn the cards over to see if you're right until you have repeated this process with both cards.

Often, people lose confidence in themselves, and when they're worried about being wrong, it blocks their psychic sense. Don't worry about being wrong; that's not the point of this exercise. Just do this activity, and you will improve your psychic eye.

## CHAPTER 8

# Does He Feel the Same Way I Do?

Many of my clients fuss over whether the men in their lives feel the same way they do. They expend a great deal of time and energy wondering about this question. Their tenacity sometimes reminds me of a dog worrying at a bone. They ask their friends, hairstylists, co-workers, and anyone else who will offer an opinion about how a man should act when he really cares about the woman in his life. One of my clients even asked a policeman because she said she needed "a man's point of view." The police officer wasn't eager to discuss my client's love life, however, since he was busy writing the report for her stolen car at the time.

The fact is that if more of my clients opened their minds— not simply to what they want but also to what their natural intuition tells them—they could avoid a lot of heartache.

## SUSAN AND MARTIN

I had been advising Susan for six months about her lawyer, Martin. According to Susan, Martin was a dashing, charismatic lawyer who had taken her breath away the instant she walked into his office to consult him about the business she was incorporating. After that first meeting, she continued to call Martin and make regular appointments so she could see him.

For Martin's part, he never indicated that he was interested in Susan. She gave him plenty of hints and opportunities to ask her out, but he never took the bait. She even made several late-afternoon appointments with him and asked if he wanted to grab some dinner afterward, but he always begged off by saying he had other plans. Susan was sure that he just needed a little more time to feel what she was feeling.

"I've never had any trouble attracting men before," Susan told me. "My ex-boyfriends always told me how they love the sexy way I dress and how confident I am. I'm sure that Martin is probably just a little intimidated by a successful woman, and he needs to realize that he's got a shot at someone like me."

"Susan, I don't think he's interested in you. I'm sorry, but I don't see the two of you in the cards," I told her.

"You're wrong, Louise. You've always steered me the right way in the past, but this time you're wrong. I can see the lust in his eyes when he looks at me. What do you think about me writing him a letter to tell him how I feel?"

As I laid the cards out on the table, there was no doubt about it: they were very negative.

"That's not a good idea. Don't do it," I told her bluntly. "You haven't made any secret of your feelings, and you've given him a number of chances to go out with you. His feelings should already be pretty clear to you by now."

"But I'm crazy about him. I have to do something," Susan said.

"Look," I told her, "if you must do something, ask him out for lunch. I feel he won't go, but give him a call and ask him. Lunch is less pressure than an evening date. Just use this as an indication of how he feels. If he says no, forget him. If he says yes, then there might be a chance. Just keep in mind that I don't see it, so you shouldn't get your hopes up."

"I'll think about it," was all Susan said before abruptly hanging up the phone.

Two weeks later, Susan called me again. She told me that she had decided to write the letter to Martin instead of asking him to lunch. It turned out to be a passionate, two-page love letter, and she had gone old school by writing it on elegant, perfumed stationery. Not having his home address, she mailed it to Martin's office. But she didn't want some secretary in the office getting her hands on such a personal letter, so she wrote "Private" on the envelope.

After mailing the letter, Susan waited for her phone to ring. She expected Martin to call and profess his love for her, but the hours and days passed without a word from him. Finally, after a week, a call came in. Susan's heart leapt when she saw on the caller ID that it was from Martin's office. But, to her dismay, it wasn't Martin's voice on the phone; it was his secretary's.

The secretary told Susan that due to a family illness, Martin had been forced to scale back his legal practice. He had given Susan's case to a different lawyer in the firm and she was supposed to contact that other attorney for all future legal services.

After recounting everything that had been going on, Susan said, "Tell me, Louise, when will he contact me about my letter?"

"Susan, he *has* contacted you about the letter. He no longer wants you as a client. It's very clear how he feels," I told her firmly. "Just forget him. He's not for you. He doesn't feel the same way you do. Someone will come into your life, but it's not him."

I knew that Susan wasn't going to listen. She might as well have been talking to me with cotton balls stuffed in her ears.

Sure enough, Susan called me again a few weeks later to tell me about her most recent interaction with Martin.

"I decided to buy him a few Hanukkah gifts. I mean, how could anyone object to that? So I got him the cutest little black yarmulke, a silver Star of David pendant, and a bottle of kosher wine," she explained. "I was on the way to give him his gifts when I saw him pulling out of the parking lot next to his office. So I followed him."

"You followed him?" I asked, startled.

"Sure I did. I wanted him to pull over so I could give him the presents. Everything was wrapped up in a nice box with a big bow," she replied reasonably, as if pursuing some man down the road in order to give him a yarmulke was the most natural thing in the world. "I didn't know what to do, so I started honking at him. He didn't stop, so I thought he didn't see me."

"How could he miss you?" I muttered.

Susan didn't respond, but just continued with her tale.

"When Martin pulled into the parking lot of the police station, I was surprised. But then I figured maybe he was just visiting one of his clients in the jail. When he jumped out of his car and ran inside, I got concerned. I thought something had to be wrong, so I grabbed my presents and followed him in. You can imagine how shocked I was when I saw him standing next to a cop, pointing at me and yelling, 'Stop her! That crazy woman is stalking me!'"

"Oh no," I said, shaking my head. "Were you arrested?"

"I explained to the cops that I was only trying to give Martin a present. The police told me to stay away from him, then let me go," Susan told me. An angry edge crept into her voice when she added, "Can you believe that? I'm starting to think Martin's a jerk."

## LESSONS LEARNED

Sometimes it's hard for people to be objective about their own behavior. They know that they don't mean any harm by calling another person or driving by his house or otherwise keeping track of him. The problem is that it's impossible to know what someone else's intentions are.

In Susan's case, the person she was interested in didn't share her affection. Unfortunately, she refused to accept that, and poor Martin had no idea why she wouldn't leave him alone. In cases like this, it's possible for the most innocent actions to be misconstrued as threatening or scary.

Susan called me several more times asking if Martin was finally going to realize what he had lost. She was very frustrated that I never saw him coming around to her way of thinking. My sincere hope is that Susan has learned her lesson and will think seriously about her behavior in the future before she frightens off another man—or ends up behind bars.

### Words of Wisdom

"Problems cannot be solved
at the same level of awareness that created them."
~Albert Einstein

# Brenda and Tom

Brenda called me one day to ask about Tom, a guy she'd been dating for a number of months. Tall, handsome, and smart, Tom was a biomedical engineer by day and Brenda's "cuddle bunny" by night. She told me at length how much attention he had paid to her in the beginning of their relationship, but lately it seemed like it was starting to peter out. Now Tom called only once a day, and she couldn't even count on seeing him every weekend. Brenda was distraught, thinking he was slipping away from her.

"At first, he was always eager to talk to me. I'd call him, and he'd get back to me in a few minutes. Now sometimes it takes him all day to call me back. He claims he's in the middle of a huge project at work where they're acquiring a new company or something, but that sounds like a load of bull to me!" Brenda told me in exasperation.

"Brenda, I feel that Tom's telling you the truth. He's just very, very busy with work right now. Don't worry. The way he's acting has nothing to do with any change in his feelings for you," I told her.

I shuffled my Tarot cards and began pulling them from the deck. Something quite interesting emerged immediately.

"Good news, Brenda," I said. "The Lovers card is in a very prominent position. That means he's crazy about you. He definitely loves you a great deal."

"Yeah, right," Brenda said sarcastically.

It was evident from her tone that Brenda was having a hard time believing that everything was going to be all right. This kind of attitude is common among women who have had bad relationship experiences in the past. It's as if they believe it's more natural to feel miserable than happy. And I knew that this kind of negative thinking could become a self-fulfilling prophecy.

"Please do me a favor," I said to Brenda. "I know you're worried about Tom, but you'd be better off if you'd think positive about your relationship. However, if you can't do that, at least make sure you don't let your fears turn into negative behavior toward him. I've seen women actually drive away their men through jealousy and suspicion. Right now, everything is fine between you two, but that doesn't mean you can't ruin it if you let your imagination run wild."

"I understand what you mean, Louise. All right, I'll be careful about what I say and do around him. But deep down inside, I'll know what's really going on."

Brenda called me back a couple weeks later. She said that things hadn't changed with Tom. He was still distant, and Brenda sounded defeated. Again, I told her that Tom was deeply in love, she didn't have anything to worry about, and she needed to try to stay positive.

"Louise, you sometimes use a crystal ball for readings, don't you?" she asked suddenly.

"Yes, I do. I always keep it near me when I'm talking to clients."

"Could you look in it for me and Tom? You say the Tarot cards show that Tom loves me, but maybe the cards aren't working. Maybe your crystal ball will show something different."

I reached up to the shelf over my desk and pulled the red velvet cloth off my crystal ball. I placed the ball and its silver stand on the table in front of me, then wiped it three times to clear the energy from my previous clients. As soon as I peered into the ball's depths, an image appeared of a man and woman kissing. I knew it was Brenda and Tom. She wore what looked like a white wedding gown.

"Brenda, you and Tom will be married," I told her simply.

"Really? What else do you see?"

"I see a diamond ring on your finger. It's quite large; three stones, as a matter of fact." The image of a dazzling diamond and gold ring filled my crystal ball. "You told me he had a good job. I guess you weren't kidding."

A few days later, Brenda called me crying. She said that Tom had told her his work was sending him to China for two weeks to conduct some training. He had no idea whether he'd have good cell phone coverage while he was there, so she shouldn't expect to hear from him while he was gone.

Brenda was in a panic. She was certain that Tom was lying and was really dumping her for another woman.

As I looked in my crystal ball, I again saw a vision of the two of them locked in a romantic embrace. Brenda wore a sleek, strapless wedding gown, and the couple stood by a horse and carriage. One detail in particular stood out: a building in the background that I could swear was a castle.

I assured Brenda that the image in my crystal ball hadn't changed. Although she was skeptical, I was unwavering in my prediction.

"I don't care what you say," she told me. "I know it's the end. I know he's got someone else. I've been burned by guys before, so I know the signs. I can tell that it's happening again."

It was four months before I heard from Brenda again. She was a completely different woman from the one I had talked to previously. She proudly announced that she and Tom were engaged.

"I've been so busy planning the wedding and house hunting, I didn't have time to call you," she said. The happiness in her voice was unmistakable.

Brenda proceeded to fill me in on all the events that had transpired since our last conversation. She told me how Tom had come home from his trip to China and asked if he could take her out to dinner at her favorite restaurant. She figured that was it. He was going to break up with her and thought she'd be less likely to make a scene in a public place.

"But as soon as we sat down, the waiter brought over a bottle of champagne that Tom had ordered beforehand. The next thing I knew, Tom was down on one knee, pulling this gorgeous ring out of his jacket and asking me to marry him. I couldn't believe it! It was like a fairy tale."

"So when's the wedding?" I asked.

"In the spring. And you haven't even heard the best part. I told Tom that ever since I was a little girl I've dreamed of getting married at Disney World, so I could feel like a princess in my wedding gown by Cinderella's Castle. I figured I'd never find a guy who would go along with such a girly idea, but Tom's into it! I've always had a fantasy about marrying a prince, and now I've found him!"

As Brenda spoke, I glanced at my crystal ball. It had turned vibrant pink, the color of love. True love.

## Lessons Learned

If Brenda had only listened to her heart and hadn't been so unsure of Tom's feelings for her, she could have saved herself a lot of heartache. The fact is that no matter how important you are to your man, he also has other demands on his time.

Don't assume that your guy is pulling away from you just because he has a full and busy life.

On the other hand, Susan in the previous story was overly confident and ignored all the signals from Martin. These two stories show that when we're trying to figure out how the object of our affection feels, we need to wipe away both self-doubt and ego. Either one can spell disaster if allowed to run rampant.

Too many of my clients let their previous relationships pollute their current efforts at love. It's important to wipe the slate clean for each new man and open our hearts and minds to the endless possibilities that life has to offer. There's no guarantee that we'll get everything we want, but previous experiences have no power over our present and future relationships unless we let them.

## Words of Wisdom

"Watch your thoughts, they become words.
Watch your words, they become actions.
Watch your actions, they become habits.
Watch your habits, they become your character.
Watch your character, it becomes your destiny."
~*Author unknown*

## JUST THE FACTS

Like Brenda in the preceding story, many women drive themselves crazy worrying about whether their boyfriends or husbands are cheating on them. While it's true that some women—and men, too—have cause for concern, the good news is that there's actually less unfaithfulness going on out there than most people think. It's also good to know that many people don't cheat simply because they deeply love their partners.

The 2007 MSNBC.com/iVillage Lust, Love & Loyalty survey collected opinions from over seventy thousand people about infidelity. The study found some interesting patterns, including the fact that cheating isn't as common as many people think it is. Only 22 percent of survey takers owned up to having participated in an affair while they were in a monogamous relationship. This number is about half what the study participants had estimated it would be. They had guessed that about 44 percent of men and 36 percent of women had probably cheated. Of course, the study revealed that there's some disagreement about what exactly constitutes cheating. For some, it's got to be actual intercourse, while others believe that kissing or online sex qualify as infidelity.

There were also significant differences between men's and women's behavior when it came to being unfaithful. Men were more likely to cheat on their partners than women, with 28 percent of married men engaging in an affair compared to 18 percent of married women. Men are more likely to engage in two or more affairs, while women typically engage in just one. Also, earning more money made men more likely to be unfaithful, while income didn't have any impact on whether a woman would have an affair.

So what keeps a person from cheating on a partner? Well, it's not having children together, because among survey participants with young children between the ages of two and five years, 16 percent of the men and 15 percent of the women were unfaithful. It's also probably not because they'd gotten caught in the past, since very few reported ever having been caught. Instead, the survey found that about 75 percent of respondents didn't cheat because they loved their partner too much. Nearly that many said they were afraid of losing their partner if they were to cheat.

The unfortunate fact is that sometimes one partner in a relationship isn't as committed as the other person, and that might lead to infidelity. However, these cases are less common than we often think. That's especially true for someone like Brenda, who had bad relationships in the past that caused her to expect the worst. Instead, it's better to think positive and play the higher probability odds that your partner is faithful and loves you very much.

## Words of Wisdom

"Who, being loved, is poor?"
~Oscar Wilde

## USING THE PSYCHIC EDGE

Thinking positively about what you want is a powerful way to draw those things to you. By the same token, if you focus on negative thoughts, you are more likely to experience those things that you don't want. So what do you do? Focus on the positive, of course.

Find five pictures that represent things you want. Try these suggestions:

1. A photo of a man you find attractive or the real-life man you're currently in love with.
2. The kind of house you want to live in with him.

3. The diamond ring or other expensive piece of jewelry you'd like him to give you.

4. The honeymoon or exotic vacation you want to go on with him.

5. The kind of car you'd like to travel in when the two of you go out together.

These suggestions may or may not appeal to you, but the important thing is to pick out the sorts of things you want to go along with the man.

Take these five pictures and spread them in a semicircle in front of you. Look at these pictures. Don't just take a glance at them; really *look* at them. Visualize yourself actually *in* the pictures and enjoying the life you're creating.

Now close your eyes and say out loud:

"I see clearly. I am focused. He is in my life. He loves me. I have everything I desire."

Repeat these statements several times. Then open your eyes and look at the pictures spread out in front of you, once again envisioning yourself as a part of the scene.

What we say, what we think, what we envision… it all comes to us. Try to do this exercise at least once a day. Choose your pictures wisely, because the point is to draw the things you want to you.

## CHAPTER 9

# Why Won't He Put More Effort into This Relationship?

How many TV sitcom episodes have you seen where the husband forgets his wedding anniversary or his wife's birthday or Valentine's Day? Meanwhile the wife has not only purchased gifts for him, but has also chilled the wine, gotten her hair done, and put on sexy lingerie. This is a tried-and-true Hollywood storyline because it rings true. Women are more likely to keep track of these relationship details than men—and men are more likely to end up in the doghouse because of it. But does that mean the problem is fair or reasonable? Maybe Mindy's and Sylvia's stories will help you decide.

## MINDY AND LEN

Technically, Mindy is not one of my clients. She's a close friend I've known for years. Still, when she was single and had boyfriend troubles, I could count on her to give me a call or arrange a lunch so we could work it out together. Now that she's married to Len, she doesn't have any dating-related complaints, but she sometimes needs to get a few things off her mind about her new husband.

One evening, I met Mindy for dinner. Len was out of town on business, so it was a nice chance for my friend and me to catch up. Our waitress had just taken drink orders when I noticed the sparkly silver bangle on Mindy's wrist.

"That's a pretty bracelet," I commented.

"Thanks. It was from Len for our anniversary," she replied as she waved her hand back and forth to make the metal catch the light.

"He has good taste."

"Oh, he didn't buy the bracelet. I did."

"But you said—" I began, confused.

"I said he gave it to me. And he sort of did. He asked me what I wanted for our anniversary, and I said jewelry. Of course, I meant that I wanted *him* to buy me jewelry. But instead, you know what I got? A gift certificate to a jewelry store. So I could go buy what I wanted, he claimed. But I know that he just didn't feel like taking the time to go shopping for me." Mindy rolled her eyes as she took a swig of the wine our waitress had brought.

"Well, at least he went to the jewelry store for the gift card, right?" I suggested.

"Hardly. He bought it online. Didn't even bother getting up from his desk."

I tried again. "But at least you got a pretty bracelet out of the deal."

"Yeah, I guess. Still, it wasn't exactly what I was expecting for our first wedding anniversary, you know? Is it so much to ask that he'd put forth a little effort when he does things for me? It's like he wants credit for doing something, but he doesn't want to have to try."

"It seems like this is about more than just the bracelet," I observed.

"It's everything. He'll be home from his business trip tomorrow, and he'll probably do what he always does when he gets back from out of town. He'll stop at the grocery store and pick up some flowers for me, then hand them over in their stupid plastic sleeve. No vase, no card, no nothing. Just 'Here, honey, take this symbol of my undying love that still has the $9.99 sticker on it.'" Mindy sighed deeply. "Does it mean anything when there was no effort put into it?"

"Please don't revoke my membership to the X Chromosome Club or anything," I began carefully, "but is it possible that Len thinks he is putting effort into getting those flowers? He has to stop at the store when he really wants to get home and relax after his trip. Maybe the two of you just define 'effort' differently."

"I guess. But it's really not enough for me. I mean, when I get him a gift, I go all out. For our anniversary, I had to go to three different malls before I found the right thing, then I had to find a card that said what I wanted and gift wrap that wasn't too girly. I cooked his favorite dinner, with candles and the whole deal. I had saved our champagne flutes from the wedding, so we drank our wine out of those. It was perfect. Then he presented me with a stinking gift card to the jewelry store. What's missing from this picture?"

"You know, this isn't the first time I've heard complaints like this," I told Mindy. "A lot of my clients feel the same way about their boyfriends and husbands. For most women, a hot date requires more than their guy dropping by with a pizza and a six-pack to watch *Monday Night Football*. Unfortunately, the guys never get why the women end up in a snit all night.

As far as the men are concerned, there's food, booze, entertainment, and the two of you are together. What more do you need?"

"So my only option is to start dating women?" Mindy joked.

"I wish you'd thought of that before I bought you and Len a wedding gift," I responded with a grin. "No, if you don't want to take such a drastic step, here's what I tell my clients: Be very clear about what you want from a man. Don't leave anything to chance. Write it down if you need to so he won't forget."

"So I have to write down that I don't want flowers in a plastic sleeve? Isn't that pretty evident?" Mindy said.

"Apparently not. And you don't have to be insulting about it. I know Len loves you and doesn't mean to make you angry when he gives you presents. I really feel he's trying, so you could give him a little gentle direction. Like maybe tell him that you want flowers arranged tastefully in a pretty vase. Tell him which florist you prefer. Be explicit, but keep it simple, because his attention span regarding flowers and things like that will be short. I had one client who got annoyed whenever her husband bought her gifts because he always bragged about how deeply discounted the presents were. She finally just told him that she didn't want to know how much her presents cost. That solved the problem."

"But that isn't what I want, either," Mindy told me. "Len should just know this stuff. He should know how to plan an evening together or buy something for me without written instructions. It's not like he's an alien who just landed on this planet."

"Unfortunately, women expect men to think like women. But they're not women. Their priorities are different. Most men just don't read into other people's actions to the same degree that women do, and I don't think there's any way to make them think like us. If you came home from work one night carrying a six-pack and a pizza, Len wouldn't care if you thought of it ten minutes ago or if you'd been planning it for a week. It wouldn't even occur to him."

Mindy nodded. "You're right. He wouldn't even ask."

"After years of talking to clients about problems like this, I've found that expecting a man to guess what you want can be a recipe for disaster. I know you don't want to have to hold Len's hand all the time, but maybe in this you have to. A little time investment now could teach him what you want, and it might pay off down the road. Maybe by the time you get to your tenth anniversary, he'll have you figured out."

"So that's the solution? Lowered expectations?" Mindy concluded.

I shrugged. "It's better than the alternative. What's the point of tying yourself up in knots about something he did— or didn't do—when it just makes you unhappy, while being completely lost on him?"

"All right, I'll give it a try. But by the time we're on our tenth anniversary, if I'm still getting flowers in those plastic sleeves, I'm going to blame you."

"That sounds fair," I agreed, picking up my wine glass.

## LESSONS LEARNED

It would be nice if the world were perfect and everything was just the way we wanted it to be. Unfortunately, the world isn't perfect, and neither are the people we share it with. Still, I talk to so many women who make themselves unhappy because they expect the men they're with to be perfect. Whether it's a boyfriend who spends every Sunday watching football from the sofa, or a fiancé who decorates his apartment like he's a breast-obsessed adolescent, or, as in Mindy's case, a husband whose idea of the ultimate romantic gift is grocery-store flowers, these guys have flaws. But the flaws aren't the real problem. The real problem is how women react to them.

What would happen if every Sunday the girlfriend just accepted that her man was out of commission, but it freed her up to go shopping with her friends? Or since the fiancée hates her future husband's decorating taste, maybe they should ask for the services of a decorator on their bridal registry. And maybe Mindy could stop seeing the inadequacies in her husband's gifts and be more grateful that he thought of her.

A good way to do this is to ask a simple question: "Why am I making myself miserable?" Next time you get tied up in an anger knot, try asking that question to remind yourself who's in control of your feelings. Hopefully it will make you let go of the negative feelings so you can arrange those last-minute flowers in a vase and enjoy their fragrance.

## Words of Wisdom

"No one saves us but ourselves. No one can and no one may. We ourselves must walk the path."

~Buddha

## SYLVIA AND JOEL

Sylvia called me one day to talk about Joel, her new boy-friend of five months. She wasted no time launching into a graphic description of Joel's behavior.

"Louise, he really is a nice guy. Probably the nicest guy I've ever gone out with. But the problem started as soon as we agreed to be exclusive with one another. He changed," Sylvia told me in exasperation.

"Changed? How?" I asked.

"He's so sloppy. For weeks I haven't seen him dressed in anything but baggy sweatpants and a big T-shirt. He doesn't care how he looks. Sure, he's clean because he showers and everything, but his hair is always messy and his beard isn't trimmed. I swear if I saw him standing on the corner and didn't know him, I'd think he was a bum."

As I peered into my crystal ball, I could actually see Joel's silhouette, baggy pants and all. He looked unkempt, but I got a lovely feeling about him as a person. He was genuinely a nice guy.

"Sylvia, clothes really don't make the man. I can see that Joel is a great guy, just like you said," I told her. "Also, I feel marriage is on the horizon for the two of you."

"Really?" She sounded surprised by my prediction. "But he's not making any effort in our relationship. His idea of an exciting date is when he comes over looking all sloppy, with a pizza in one hand and his gym bag in the other. Then he flops down on my couch to eat, watch TV, cuddle with me, and fart."

"What?" I thought I had heard her incorrectly.

"That's right, I said fart." Sylvia chuckled. "He doesn't hold back at all. As soon as we became an official couple, he really started to let 'em rip. Can you believe it? He passes gas, then he looks at me and laughs. He's not ashamed one bit."

I couldn't help but smile at the scenario Sylvia described. I explained to her that Joel wasn't all that unusual. The problem she described was one that I'd heard many times from my female clientele in the past.

"Louise, how can I get him to try harder to impress me? Is it so much to ask that he should dress nicer and stop the farting?" Sylvia asked.

As I laid out my Tarot cards, there was only one clear answer. I had to tell her the truth.

"Sylvia, I'm sorry to tell you this, but I see that Joel is so comfortable with you and loves you so much that he thinks it's okay to be himself. As far as he's concerned, he's making an effort where it counts: by treating you well and spending time with you. To him, wearing a suit and tie is meaningless. It's just window dressing."

"Window dressing, huh?" Sylvia mused. "It's funny you said that. He uses those exact words when he describes people on TV or strutting around the mall wearing fancy clothes and makeup. He says he can't imagine why they waste all their time and money on 'window dressing.' He says you can put lipstick on a pig, but it's still a pig."

I grinned. Joel was a funny, practical sort of guy. I liked him. But Sylvia was my client, not Joel, so I had to give her some advice.

"You can buy him some different clothes as a gift," I told her. "He'll wear them sometimes to make you happy, but the sweats and T-shirts are what he's comfortable in. You can get him some medicine for his gas, and he might take it sometimes if you bug him about it. He really is a wonderful guy who wants to make you happy. However, if you can't accept the no-frills, what-you-see-is-what-you-get part of his personality, then you probably should move on, because this is going to be a constant source of aggravation in your life."

Sylvia wasn't happy to hear what I was telling her. She said she liked Joel's personality too much to let him go without a fight. However, she didn't agree that his behavior was a sign of how much he loved her. Instead, she believed that it showed he didn't care about her feelings. In essence, she had a hard time accepting anything that I was seeing.

"I think your crystal ball needs a tune-up," was the last thing she said to me before she hung up. I felt bad about not being able to tell her what she wanted to hear, but I couldn't lie about what I saw.

Then one day a few months later, I heard a bubbly voice on the phone.

"Louise, this is Sylvia. Do you remember me? I had the gassy, sloppy boyfriend?"

I laughed and told her that I remembered her very well.

"I just had to call and tell you. Joel and I are engaged!" she cried.

"I'm so happy to hear it! I told you marriage was on the horizon."

"Yes, you did. And I didn't believe you. I'm sorry about that," she said.

"No need to apologize," I said. "I'm just glad it all worked out."

"It sure did. One night Joel came over with a bottle of wine and my favorite Italian beef sandwiches. While we were watching TV, he reached into the pocket of his sweatpants and pulled out a little blue box. There was a huge diamond engagement ring inside! He said, 'Nothing but the best for my lady.' He's so romantic," Sylvia said with a sigh.

"Is everything else okay between the two of you? No complaints?" I hinted.

"Everything is wonderful! I don't even notice his sloppy clothes anymore, or the gas," she said. "And the big advantage I discovered is that he doesn't care what I look like. I can come home from work and throw my hair in a ponytail and slip into flannel pajamas, and he's just as happy as if I were dressed in an evening gown and a tiara. It feels terrific to just totally be myself around another person."

## LESSONS LEARNED

We judge other people's actions by our own standards. Sylvia had a set idea of how a man who is interested in a woman should act. But when she opened her mind and looked beyond physical appearance, a bright new future opened up to her. Joel's apparent lack of effort in their relationship didn't represent his disinterest in her. Instead, it showed how close he felt to her and demonstrated his priorities. Luckily, Sylvia was eventually able to look past the sweatpants and into the heart of her prince. And she even came to realize that his relaxed attitude held big benefits for her, too.

### Words of Wisdom

"Women are made to be loved, not understood."

~Oscar Wilde

# Just the Facts

Women gauge how much they mean to their men by using all kinds of scales. Some of those measures make more sense than others. Some women look at how much time their man spends with them, or how often they have sex, or whether he ever brings her flowers. For other women, it's not an objective measure, but more of a comparative one: What do her friends' husbands/boyfriends do for them, and how does the man in her life stack up?

But does the amount of time or money a man spends on his significant other really indicate how much he cares? Or does it predict something else entirely? Surprisingly, science comes to the rescue with an answer to this question.

Researchers at Rutgers University were curious about what factors influence how much money a man will spend on an engagement ring. As a starting point for their 2010 study, "Applications of Signaling Theory to Contemporary Human Courtship," they noted that in both animal and human groups it's common for gifts to be offered to a prospective mate. The value of those gifts tended to increase as "mate quality" increased.

What, you might ask, is mate quality? It varies by species, sex, and culture, but in the case of the humans studied by Rutgers researchers, high-quality female mates were young and/or had a high income, while high-quality male mates had high incomes. The idea is that young women are best able to produce babies, and rich men are best able to support them financially.

The researchers then sent questionnaires to recently married couples to find out who bought engagement rings, how much they spent, how old the couple was, and how much they earned. The results showed that the most expensive engagement rings were generally given to younger brides and to brides with higher incomes. Not surprisingly, the men with the highest incomes gave more expensive rings to their prospective brides.

These results aren't a surprise. The more money a man has, the nicer the ring he can afford—and maybe the younger and hotter the woman he can buy it for.

It's important to remember that these findings don't say anything about how committed either the husband or the wife is to the relationship. Just because a man spends a fortune on a massive rock doesn't mean he's putting a lot of effort into the relationship. It could simply mean that he's got the cash to spend. And a poor man who buys an inexpensive ring might be head over heels in love, but he doesn't have the bank account to prove it.

## USING THE PSYCHIC EDGE

Sometimes people suppress their intuition or psychic feelings because they're afraid to acknowledge an answer that might be negative. This is a common problem for women who want to know whether the men in their lives really care. So what women need is a method to draw out their own intuition to decipher men's feelings. The following activity is one of many in this book that can help you uncover what your intuition is telling you.

For this exercise, you will need a pad of paper and a pen. Sit in a comfortable chair, close your eyes, and think of a question you want the answer to. For example, you can ask "Does he love me?" or "Will he marry me?" With your eyes closed, take the pen and move it across the paper in any fashion you feel, creating squiggly lines, letters, doodles, or anything else in any direction your hand moves. Keep your eyes closed, and don't look at the paper until you're done writing. Loosening the control that your conscious mind usually holds over your body will help open your psychic unconscious.

When you feel you're done, look carefully at the doodles on your paper. What do they say to you? How have you answered your question? Again, relax your conscious mind to interpret what you see. You might be surprised at the answers revealed to you. The more often you do this exercise, the better you will get at unlocking your unconscious mind.

## CHAPTER 10

# How Can I Get Him to Change?

It's hard to get a man—or anyone, for that matter—to change his behavior. You fell in love with him the way he is, so after you're involved in a relationship it's tough to turn around and say, "You're perfect! Except for a few little things…" If the relationship means a lot to him, he might try to make some changes in order to please you, but most people eventually revert to old patterns. Also, it's important to recognize the difference between men who are simply too broken to fix and those who just need a tune-up.

## Words of Wisdom

"I Love You, You're Perfect, Now Change."
~Joe DiPietro

## DOROTHY AND DUKE

"Do you think Duke stole my credit card?" Dorothy sobbed into the phone.

"Yes, I do," I told Dorothy simply as I studied the cards spread out before me. There was no doubt in my mind that he took the card.

"But he promised me last time he stole some of my checks that he'd never steal from me again. What can I do? How can I make him change?" she moaned.

Over the course of the past year, Dorothy had asked me these same questions a dozen times. She was smart and pretty and owned a successful dry cleaning business. She also had an unfortunate attraction to bad boys. The first time she laid eyes on Duke, he was standing onstage at a local bar, belting out a tune on karaoke night. Instantly she felt the magic.

Duke had ten tattoos, plus piercings on his nose, ears, and right eyebrow. He also had five kids, three ex-wives, a drug problem, and a criminal record. What he didn't have was a job. Dorothy insisted that he had a good heart and lots of potential.

"Duke's not all bad," she had told me more than once. "He never misses his kids' birthdays. Deep down he's a good guy."

"Dorothy, Duke shows up at his kids' parties because he knows there'll be beer there for the grown-ups," I reminded her. "Trust me. This man can't be fixed. He'll never change. I've told you this many times. There is someone out there for you who's much better. And he won't steal from you."

"But I want Duke," Dorothy said quietly before she hung up.

I didn't hear from Dorothy again for several months. When she called, the first thing she told me was that she had let Duke move in with her.

"At first, he seemed like he really was trying to get his act together," she said with a sniffle. "But that didn't last, and now he's worse than ever. I came home yesterday and Duke was gone. So were my laptop, TV, iPod, and diamond tennis bracelet. He left me a note saying his brother was sick and he'd be gone for a few days."

"Have you tried calling him?" I asked.

"I've left messages, but he won't call me back. Louise, I don't know what to do. What do you see?"

I sighed and turned over a few Tarot cards. "Dorothy, let me ask you a question. What will this man have to do to make you realize that he's not going to change?"

There was silence on the other end of the phone. Finally Dorothy whispered, "I—I don't know."

"Okay, here's what I think you should do. First, cut off all contact with him," I said. Dorothy yelped and started to protest, but I interrupted her. "You might not want to hear this, but I'm looking in my crystal ball, and the next step in your relationship is physical violence. Break up with Duke now before that happens." I could feel that it was important to tell Dorothy what I saw, even though it was painful to her. Any future she had with Duke didn't look good.

"Oh no, Duke might have some faults, but I know he'd never hurt me," Dorothy insisted. After a few more minutes of denials about Duke's behavior, she hung up.

Over the course of the next few months, Dorothy called me periodically. She was intermittently angry, frustrated, or in tears over Duke's treatment of her. Every time she called, I told her to get out of the relationship. Then one day she called and sounded different. There was sadness in her voice, but there was also a new confidence.

"Well, it's over," Dorothy announced.

"With Duke? What happened? Did he hurt you?" I asked.

"He tried. He got mad at me one night. He was drunk and wanted me to go out and buy him more beer, but I said no. Then he took my car keys so he could drive to the store himself. I ran outside to stop him, and he actually tried to run me over in the driveway!"

"Oh, Dorothy! Are you all right?"

"Yes, I got out of the way, but that was enough for me. I called the police, kicked Duke's drunken butt out of my house, and ended our relationship for good."

"I'm so glad you're all right!" I told her. "And of course I'm glad you finally got rid of Duke."

"Me, too. I just wish I'd listened to you sooner."

"Better late than never. I hope he hasn't been bothering you since you broke up with him." I knew that harassment was tragically common in cases like these.

"Fortunately, no. I think that when the police threw him in jail, and I not only wouldn't bail him out but wouldn't even take his call, he got the hint." Dorothy paused, then added, "I have to say that I'm so much happier without Duke in my life. I finally have peace."

## Lessons Learned

It feels good to have an optimistic view of human nature and people's ability to improve themselves, but sometimes that optimistic view is simply delusional. Was there some chance that Duke might someday be able to pull his life together and become the man Dorothy wanted him to be? Maybe. But that wasn't going to happen while he was with Dorothy and definitely not until he fully committed himself to doing it. There was no evidence in his behavior that he wanted to make himself a better person. The sad fact is that sometimes when you see the guy in your life self-destructing, the best thing you can do is get out of the way so you don't catch any shrapnel.

## PATRICIA AND LEON

Patricia called me in exasperation. Leon was a good-looking, confident drummer in a rock band. She was crazy about him, but he had a terrible attitude. The fact that he had women throwing themselves at him every time he was onstage didn't improve his demeanor. He was actually getting worse.

"He's so obnoxious. I love him, but sometimes I can't stand him," she admitted.

"Why don't you tell me about the things he does that bother you," I suggested.

"Try this one on for size," she replied. "Leon likes to get his testosterone levels tested once a month. He bragged to me that his doctor told him how high his levels are, higher than any man he'd ever seen. Ever since then, Leon's been telling me what a stud he is. And then there's how he's always asking me to tell him how big his penis is. If I don't immediately tell him that his penis is the biggest one I've ever seen, he has a long face all day."

Some of the stories Patricia told me about Leon brought a smile to my face. Leon loved to take off his shirt and dance to Village People songs in front of a full-length mirror. Before he'd go play a gig, he'd always pose for Patricia and ask how he looked. If she didn't tell him he was a super-hot stud and the best lover she'd ever been with, he'd give her the silent treatment. When Patricia watched something on TV that had a handsome man in it, Leon would get jealous and stand in front of the screen, asking if he was good-looking enough to have his own show.

"What can I do about him? How can I get him to change?" she asked me in exasperation. "He's a great guy in a lot of ways. He's an awesome musician, and he's funny, and it's always exciting to be with him. This crap is getting on my nerves, though."

I flipped the Tarot cards and instantly saw something interesting: Leon was insecure. His behavior toward Patricia was all bravado. Inside, he felt unsure of himself and was worried that she'd figure out he wasn't good enough for her. He loved Patricia and needed her approval more than anything else. This information made it easy to tell her how to handle Leon.

"Patricia, don't wait for him to ask you how he looks before giving him a compliment. Say something flattering before he asks you, and do it often. He needs confirmation from you that he's the greatest. Yours is the opinion he values the most."

"Well, I'll try, but I hate the idea of giving him any compliments because he's so arrogant already," she told me. "Won't I just be feeding his ego?"

"Remember that the way he acts isn't about arrogance; it's insecurity. Maybe remembering that will make it easier for you to help him."

The next time Patricia called, she happily informed me that Leon was much better.

"He's not nearly as obnoxious as he was before. Actually, he's getting sweeter all the time. He stopped with that ridiculous testosterone testing, and lately he's been writing love songs for me. He says he needs a whole set of them for his band to play at our wedding."

"Congratulations! I predict you'll be married in October," I said. "And I also predict that he'll spend your entire wedding day telling you how beautiful you look."

## LESSONS LEARNED

Leon wanted desperately to please Patricia; he just had no clue how to go about it. Fortunately, when Patricia discovered the foundation of his problems, it became clear that they weren't insurmountable. With a little effort on Patricia's part, she was able to help turn Leon's behavior around. This story is in contrast to Dorothy and Duke's. In that case, Duke was too broken to change in any lasting way. His problems had nothing to do with his feelings for Dorothy; they had everything to do with him being a self-centered, sociopathic user. Maybe years of intense psychotherapy could have helped him, but his girlfriend was way out of her depth.

When trying to figure out if it's possible to get someone to change, you should look at how severe the problem is. Also consider whether your man will want to make the change in order to please you. Your intuition can be very useful for this purpose, and you should also study his behavior to determine how important your feelings are to him. Another consideration—and one that's hard to be objective about—is whether the change you desire is really beneficial for your man. For instance, maybe you'd like him to go antiquing with you on Sundays rather than watching football. But what if he needs to decompress from his stressful weekday job, and football does that for him?

Finally, please keep in mind that sometimes it's impossible to get your man to change even the most minor behavior. He might not be motivated because he gets something out of his behavior that you don't understand or he might not be committed enough to the relationship to make an effort. But when all is said and done, if a man just needs a tune-up, there's little risk in trying to get him to change. On the other hand, if he needs a whole new engine, it's better just to turn him in for a new model.

## Words of Wisdom

"We are not the same persons this year as last; nor are those we love. It is a happy chance if we, changing, continue to love a changed person."
~W. Somerset Maugham

## JUST THE FACTS

Women are often attracted to successful men. Their power, money, and fame are why movie stars, professional athletes, and politicians are never at a loss for female companionship. Successful men typically display characteristics of what are known as *alpha males*. This term refers to male animals of many species that are geared to be dominant in their social groups.

It can be easy for a woman to fall in love with an alpha male. He's confident and aggressive and goes after what he wants. When the couple is dating, it's fun to watch him take charge of situations and make decisions about where to go and what to do. He could make a woman feel like the heroine in a romance novel. But the thrill doesn't last forever.

Once the couple is married and settled down, the woman probably wants to relax a little. She wants to kick back together on a Sunday and go to a movie or walk through a forest preserve, or maybe take the kids to the zoo. But the alpha male can't seem to do that. Everything is a competition, from keeping the lawn greener than the neighbors' to pushing the children to succeed at every sport they try. And after a while it starts to drive even the most tolerant woman nuts.

The irony is that qualities that initially attracted the woman to her husband—including his confidence, success, and drive—are now the things that are driving her crazy. And now she wants him to change. Although getting a partner to change is often a frustrating and futile effort, there are some very good reasons why an alpha male should make an attempt to dial down his dominant personality a bit.

The downside of being an alpha male was demonstrated in a 2011 study of baboons, "Life at the Top: Rank and Stress in Wild Male Baboons," conducted by researchers at Duke and Princeton Universities. They found that alpha male baboons had access to the best food and opportunities to mate with the most females, but that success came at a high price. Those baboons also had high levels of cortisol in their bodies, which is a hormone produced when animals are under stress.

The males just below alphas in a social hierarchy are known as betas. They get as much food and sex as the alphas, but they have much less stress. This is probably because they don't have to constantly deal with other males challenging their position.

This baboon study supports the notion that while alpha males attract females and are driven to succeed, they might be unable to enjoy their success. If a woman marries a man who's successful at work and able to purchase a nice home and car, she might think it's time for him to relax and enjoy a comfortable life with his family. But he might have trouble toning down his competitive instincts. It's vital that he does, though, because the stress hormones can lead to increased risk of illness, including heart disease and a weakened immune system.

So if you're involved with an alpha male, how do you keep your guy from working himself into an early grave? Exercise is often recommended as a means of burning extra energy and lowering stress. Also, relaxation techniques like meditation and yoga are successful for some men. Of course, these might be extra challenging for alpha males because they're not competitive activities, so they don't come naturally. On the other hand, since more competition is the last thing an alpha male needs, they could be just what the doctor ordered.

## Words of Wisdom

"Power is the ultimate aphrodisiac."
~Henry Kissinger

### USING THE PSYCHIC EDGE

Sometimes our man exhibits behavior that bothers us, and we're not even sure why. We also might not know whether it's possible to stop the behavior. This exercise is designed to help you identify your own underlying feelings about what you'd like your partner to change.

Put on some soft music and lie down on a bed or sofa. Allow yourself to relax, and concentrate on your breathing. When you feel comfortable, direct your mind back to the most recent time your significant other did something that irritated or upset you. Recall the conversation or his actions to the best of your ability. What did he say or do? How did you respond? How did each step in this encounter make you feel?

When you have a firm picture of the events in your mind, try to consider why the situation made you so upset. Maybe he made an insensitive comment about your weight. Why did that bother you so much? Was it because he himself is overweight, so he has no right to talk, or because you were teased about your weight as a child and are now particularly sensitive about it? Maybe you're just tired of him embarrassing you in public. Use your intuition to uncover why this bothered you so much.

Next, ask yourself why he did it. Was he trying to upset you? Did he have no clue that you were sensitive about your weight? Again, use your intuition. Deep down you already know why he behaves the way he does; you just need to unlock the truth. You also know whether it's possible or to your advantage to spend the time trying to change him. For instance, he might simply be unaware that he offended you, so telling him about it might be all it takes to make him think before he speaks next time.

Feel free to practice this exercise as long or as often as you need. You'll be surprised at the insights you'll uncover.

SECTION THREE

# Keeping Love

## CHAPTER 11

# Commitment, Part One: Why Hasn't He Proposed Yet?

Congratulations! You've found a guy and you've fallen for each other. It's time for happily ever after, right? Not necessarily. There are an awful lot of pitfalls that can trip up true love before you grow old together on a front porch in his-and-hers rocking chairs. This section of the book focuses on some common relationship speed bumps, like fear of commitment, betrayal, and attempts to keep the romance alive. We'll start with a commitment issue that I hear about from so many clients who are in search of a long-term relationship.

Whether a woman has been dating her guy for six weeks, six months, or six years, there's always that question at the back of her mind about whether they're going to get married someday. Unfortunately, it's generally up to the man to decide whether to propose. Sure, in this modern world, there's no reason the woman can't take the bull by the horns and pop the question herself, but very few women are willing to take such a nontraditional leap. Plus, many a woman has long dreamed of the day when the love of her life gets down on one knee and presents her with a diamond as big as a walnut. It's hard to give up on that ideal.

That means too many women find themselves wondering what their man is waiting for. And it's not like they aren't committed to each other in other aspects of their lives. Maybe they've been together for years. Maybe they live together. Maybe they've got kids together. Still, the proposal is nowhere to be found. So what's the problem? Why are the four little words "Will you marry me?" so hard to say for some men?

## Words of Wisdom

"Never get married in the morning,
because you never know who you'll meet that night."
~Paul Hornung

## COURTNEY AND JAMES

As soon as I picked up the phone, there was a deep sigh on the other end.

"Oh, Louise, I feel lousy. Can you tell me if I did the right thing?"

"It's good to hear from you, Courtney. It's been about a year, hasn't it?" I asked. Courtney had been a regular client of mine up until she started dating a new guy and her calls tapered off. I had assumed that not hearing from her meant things were going well in her life. I had a pretty strong idea why she was calling me now, and it wasn't good.

"Yeah, I'm sorry it's been so long, but I was really busy. And things seemed to be going so well." There was another deep sigh on Courtney's end.

"But now?" I asked. "I take it the relationship ended badly with that man you were with last year?"

"It did. And I had such high hopes for him, too. I thought he was 'the one.' Last Christmas was our one-year dating anniversary, and I thought for sure he'd pop the question. There was even a little jewelry box wrapped up under his Christmas tree."

"You thought it was a ring?"

"Of course. It was the right size. Then on Christmas morning, he handed me a big box instead. It was a throw blanket decorated with the Dallas Cowboys logo."

"That was quite a disappointment. Who was the jewelry box for?" I asked.

"His mother. She's got one of those charm bracelets, and he bought her a charm to go on it."

"Okay, so Christmas was a bust, but that was six months ago. Something just happened to make you so upset," I said.

"You're right, and I'm trying to figure out if I'm the idiot or if he is," Courtney said.

"I'm sure neither of you is an idiot. If anything, you're both confused and hurt. Why don't you tell me what happened?"

"I got tired of waiting is what happened. We'd been together for a year and a half without a word from him about getting married or having kids or moving in together or anything. That's eighteen months of my life, with my clock ticking. So finally when my birthday came and went without a ring, I told James we were through."

"And what did he say?"

"He said, 'Why does this keep happening to me?' Those were his exact words. I asked him what he meant, and he said that women were always breaking off long-term relationships with him and he didn't know why."

"Really?" I said. "He acted confused about why women break up with him?"

"That's right," Courtney said. "So I asked him how many women he's had this problem with, and he said every single one he's been in a long-term relationship with. His last girlfriend was with him for six years before she called it quits. The one before that was three years. So I asked if he'd ever asked any of them to marry him."

"And what did he say?"

"He said no. He was almost fifty years old, never been married, and never seriously considered getting engaged. And he was confused about why women break up with him. What's wrong with this guy?"

I was surprised that James had pretended to be baffled by his string of break-ups. I strongly felt that he knew exactly what the problem was. Then it occurred to me.

"Courtney, listen to me," I said. "You didn't do anything wrong by breaking up with James. And he wasn't actually confused about why women break up with him. I don't suppose the two of you have seen each other since you broke up?"

"Well, yeah, we've gotten together a few times. He seemed so lonely, I didn't want to just dump him and leave him alone. He wanted to talk so we could discuss how he could get out of this pattern he's fallen into."

"And I suppose that sometimes you end up doing more than talking?" I prompted.

Courtney paused, then said, "Um, yeah. But we were always really compatible, you know, in the bedroom. I mean, what's the harm?"

"There's no harm, Courtney, as long as you know what you're getting into," I told her. "But the fact is that James knows why women break up with him; he just doesn't want to do anything about it. I feel that he likes being single. He doesn't want to get married. But he does like you. He likes all the women he's been in long relationships with. And he likes the sex he gets while he's part of a couple."

"So why does he want to keep getting together to talk about the break-ups?" Courtney asked.

"Because he wants to hold on to the benefits of being with you for as long as possible. Like I said, he likes you and enjoys spending time with you. But he's not going to want to get married anytime soon. I think you made the right choice breaking up with him if your goal is marriage. So if I were you, I'd cut ties with James once and for all and go find a man who does want a real commitment." Then I paused and added, "And consider yourself lucky that it didn't take you six years to figure out that you and James were headed in different directions."

## LESSONS LEARNED

Some people just don't want to get married. James, for instance, liked the companionship and the sex and all the other trappings of a relationship, but a house and kids and joint bank accounts weren't his style. So he managed to figure out a way to get exactly what he wanted in a relationship without any of the stuff he didn't want.

This would have been fine if the women he dated had been on the same page with him. There are plenty of women in the world who don't want strings attached, either. Sadly, he didn't find any of those. He dated women who were looking for strings. And they grew dissatisfied when they realized they weren't getting what they wanted out of the relationship.

It's a shame that so many women wasted so much of their time waiting for James to do something he was never going to do: propose. Courtney put up with it for only eighteen months, but that was still a year and a half that she could have spent with a man who was giving her what she wanted in a relationship, just like she was giving him what he wanted. It's appropriate to step back from your relationship sometimes and evaluate it honestly. Ask yourself: Are my needs being met? And if they're not, don't wait years before doing something about it.

Also, keep in mind that it's perfectly appropriate for a woman to initiate a conversation about marriage if her guy doesn't broach the subject first. She doesn't have to propose or anything, but after you've been dating for a while, it's not unreasonable to ask the question "Do you see yourself getting married someday?" Yes, it might be embarrassing. Yes, it might feel uncomfortable if you think the man ought to make the first move. Yes, you might get an answer from him that you don't like. But isn't feeling a little discomfort or embarrassment worth finding out if you and the man in your life have the same objectives? If Courtney and the other women who dated James had only made their needs clear earlier in their relationships, they could have avoided wasting a lot of time.

### Words of Wisdom

"A man in love is incomplete until he has married.
Then he's finished."
~Zsa Zsa Gabor

# Maggie and Sam

The first time I talked to Maggie, she was in a terrible state of agitation. The more she described the situation with her boyfriend, Sam, the more short-tempered and upset she got. "We've been going out for two years now and he hasn't popped the question yet! All my friends are engaged. They've got engagement rings and everything! I just feel like exploding! Last weekend a group of us girls got together for lunch, and they were all showing off their rings. I could tell how sorry they felt for me. I was the only one without a ring!"

Maggie's voice dropped in despair. "I was so humiliated. I couldn't stand their pity. They kept saying things like, 'Don't worry, Maggie, it'll be your turn soon.' It was all I could do to sit through that awful lunch and listen to them going on about wedding planners and gowns."

As I looked into my crystal ball, I saw some unpleasant visions. One showed a woman being pushed through a doorway, and another was a ring being pulled off a finger, and still another was a woman in tears. These pictures represented bad endings to relationships; I could feel the anger and pain of the people involved. At that moment, I felt very close to these future events, as if I were there as these scenarios were playing out.

"Well, Maggie," I began, "your friends might have the rings, but they really don't have the men. Don't be jealous of them. I don't feel they'll be engaged for very long, and those weddings will never happen."

"Jealous!" Maggie cried. "I'm not jealous! I just don't like that all my friends are getting the guys they love, but I'm not. I'm being left behind."

"Believe me when I say that Sam loves you. He's just waiting for the right time to propose because he wants to be more financially stable."

"What do you mean? Sam's doing fine. He's got a good job and a nice apartment. What more does he need?"

"Your boyfriend is a responsible guy," I told her. "You're lucky to have him. Your friends aren't going to be so lucky, I'm sorry to say. As a matter of fact, you'll be married sooner than any of them. I believe he'll propose within the next six months."

As if she hadn't heard anything else I'd said, Maggie yelled into the phone, "Six months! You've got to be kidding!" Then she hung up without another word.

A few months later, I wasn't surprised when Maggie called me back.

"Louise, do you remember me? This is Maggie, and my boyfriend's name is Sam," she said shyly.

"Yes, I remember you very well," I replied.

"Look, I'm really sorry," she began. "I was in a bad mood when I called last time. I shouldn't have taken it out on you."

I smiled, knowing that she had some news for me.

"I had to call you," Maggie said. "Remember how all my friends were engaged last time we talked? Well, you won't believe what happened. My one friend thought she'd surprise her fiancé and stop by his apartment when she got off work a couple hours early. When he answered the door, my friend saw another woman inside. Wow, let me tell you, what a scene! My friend yelled and screamed and forced her way into the apartment. She threatened the other woman and refused to leave, so her fiancé called the police. The police had to physically eject her from the apartment, but then she fought with the cops so much that they arrested her."

Maggie sounded sympathetic to her friend's plight, but I could feel that she was also pleased that she wasn't the only one who wasn't engaged.

"I'm sorry to hear about what happened to your friend, but now do you understand what I told you before about how things aren't always the way they look?" I asked.

"Boy, you sure were right about that. Another one of my friends also had to call off her wedding. Her fiancé told her that he didn't want to marry her anymore. When she put up a fuss, he actually pulled the ring right off her finger! The worst part was that he'd been lying to her the whole time. Turns out he realized he's gay and he'd been dating some guy for months! He's going to exchange my friend's diamond for a men's ring so he can propose to his boyfriend."

"I know it's painful for them right now, but I hope your friends understand that they're lucky they figured out the truth before marrying these men," I told her. "You, on the other hand, have a great guy, and he's just taking a little longer than you'd like."

"Thank you, Louise. I know you're right," she told me cheerfully. Then she added with an embarrassed laugh, "Of course, it's easier for me to wait for Sam now since all my friends aren't walking down the aisle before me."

## Lessons Learned

It often happens that we don't get what we want at the very moment we want it. That was Maggie's problem. It wasn't that her relationship with Sam was flawed; it just wasn't moving at the exact pace she would have liked. But rather than be patient and enjoy her time with him, she worried about what others thought and focused her energy on trying to keep up with them.

Over the next several months, Maggie checked in with me regularly and updated me on the status of not only her relationship but also those of her friends. As it turned out, all of her girlfriends broke up with the guys they were engaged to. It took Sam longer to propose, but when he finally did, he was sincere. The first time that Maggie and her friends walked down the aisle together, it was Maggie who wore the white gown while her unattached friends wore peach bridesmaid dresses. Sometimes the best things in life take time and are worth waiting for.

## Words of Wisdom

"If you want a happy ending, that depends, of course, on where you stop your story."
~Orson Welles

## JUST THE FACTS

Most American children are raised with the notion that when they grow up, they'll get to choose their own spouse. The whole process can be messy and heartbreaking as young adults meet, date, and, if they're lucky, marry someone they love. In an ideal world, the trouble would be worth it if all couples got to enjoy a happily ever after together.

Unfortunately, in the United States, half of all marriages end in divorce—which means happily ever after isn't as common as fairy tales would have us believe. So if falling in love leaves something to be desired as a method for finding a life partner, what's the alternative?

In many cultures around the world, arranged marriages are the norm, while love matches are both rare and frowned upon. The idea behind an arranged match is that the families of the prospective bride and groom are more objective and will make a better choice than the young, inexperienced couple. Also, in these societies, marriage has traditionally been viewed as an economic union of two families rather than just the marriage of two individuals. That means it might make sense for elders in the family to have input into marital decisions.

While the idea of an arranged marriage might be strange or even offensive to many young people in Western cultures, these unions have something to recommend them. Specifically, divorce rates are very low in countries where arranged marriages are the norm. In fact, India's divorce rate is just over 1 percent, which is the lowest among the world's large nations. The highest divorce rates are in nations that are dominated by love matches, like the United States, Sweden, and the United Kingdom.

Why the differences in divorce rates? One theory is that in societies where people date in search of true love, they develop an idealized view of what it will be like when they find "the one" or their perfect soulmate. Such romantic notions can easily be dashed, which leads to dissatisfaction and, often, divorce. In arranged marriages, there are fewer preconceived notions about finding a soulmate. People can hope to fall in love with their spouse over time, but disillusionment is less of a threat.

On the other hand, it's possible that some countries might have low divorce rates not because couples are happy together but because there's a tremendous social stigma associated with divorce. According to a 2011 article in the *Huffington Post,* "India's Divorce Rate Rising," divorce in India has traditionally been something to be ashamed of, and having one in the family could even result in future difficulty finding spouses for other children. That's beginning to change, however, and India's divorce rates are beginning to creep up, particularly in urban areas. In addition, women in India now have better job opportunities than in the past, so they don't have to tolerate abusive marriages just because they're financially dependent on their husbands.

Of course, there could also be a farfetched explanation for why arranged marriages often last longer than love matches. What if maybe, just maybe, when it comes to choosing mates for their children, mother and father really do know best?

## Using the Psychic Edge

There's an old saying, "The grass is always greener on the other side of the fence." In Maggie and Sam's case, that saying was so true. Maggie saw what she thought her friends had and assumed that their engagements were better than the relationship she had with her boyfriend, Sam. What she didn't know was that her friends' relationships were far from perfect, while hers was going strong.

Maggie made a common mistake. It's easy to think that everyone else's life is perfect, because people tend to put the most positive face on things for others. Maggie's friends weren't about to discuss the problems they had with their fiancés, but they freely played up the engagement rings and wedding plans. So how do you keep from falling into the booby trap of envy, like Maggie did? Try this exercise to help you feel grateful for the things you have instead of focusing on things you don't have.

Sit down with a sheet of paper and a pen. Think about something in your life that you're grateful for and write it down. Maybe it's your boyfriend or husband, if you've got one. Maybe your kids. Maybe your job. Maybe you're grateful for the house or apartment where you're writing this list. Continue making a list of things that you appreciate in your life. Write down anything that makes you happy about your life, no matter how small or insignificant it might seem to someone else. This is *your* list.

Let your psychic intuition run loose while you're making this list. Your intuition will tell you what's really important in your life. It will also identify those things that *aren't* important, because those won't be on the list. When you're finished, put the list in a prominent spot where you can see it regularly. Don't be afraid to add to it when you think of something that belongs there.

Next time you're feeling down about any aspect of your life, take a look at your list and feel gratitude for all the wonderful things you've got. Whenever you feel envious of something that someone else has that you don't, ask yourself whether you'd even bother putting that thing on your list if you had it. Let your intuition guide you in answering that question. It always knows what's really meaningful for you, even if you sometimes forget.

Also, if you decide that you really do want something that you don't already have, it's possible to draw that object or person to you using the visualization technique presented in chapter 8. Then once you've got it, remember to put it on your gratitude list and feel appreciation for it regularly.

## Words of Wisdom

"Jealousy lives upon doubts. It becomes madness or ceases entirely as soon as we pass from doubt to certainty."
~François de la Rochefoucauld

## CHAPTER 12

# Commitment, Part Two: Why Won't He Set a Wedding Date?

In any relationship, there are different levels of commitment, and on the Commitment Meter, marriage is at the top. Is it any wonder that even people who are engaged get nervous when it comes to actually walking down that long aisle? This chapter focuses on different ways that a bride-to-be's journey to the altar can go astray.

## BETHANY AND PAUL

"Every time I talk to my mother, she asks when Paul and I are getting married. We've been engaged for two years and don't even have a date!"

"You and Paul are in college in different cities, didn't you say?" I asked.

"Yes, he's in medical school and I'm finishing a master's, but there's no reason we can't start planning. Look at my sister Janice. She got a ring from her guy after dating for only six months, and they already have the church and reception hall and everything. I can't help but wonder, 'When's my turn?' You know what I mean, Louise?"

"Yes, but you know that every relationship has its own timing. What works for one couple isn't always going to work for another." I looked at the Tarot cards in front of me. It was clear that Paul wasn't ready to walk down the aisle yet, and he was getting annoyed with Bethany's constant hints. He wanted to be with her, but he didn't want to become a husband until he had the means to support a wife. Plus I couldn't tell whether Bethany's motivation was really to marry Paul or just to get her family off her back. The key was to get both of these messages across to my client without getting her so angry that she stopped listening.

Bethany blew out a deep sigh on the other end of the phone. "Well, it doesn't matter because Paul's stopped calling me. I keep leaving him messages, but he ignores them."

"What do you say in these messages you leave?" I asked.

"Just that we need to talk. He can't keep avoiding this conversation about where our relationship is going. Ever since my sister got engaged, it's gotten embarrassing. I mean, Paul and I have been together for years! He's got to talk to me."

I was silent for a moment as I studied the cards in front of me. Bethany had clearly done serious harm to her relationship.

"It sounds like he is talking to you," I said gently, "just not in words. His actions tell you where he's at right now."

"But why can't we talk about it? I want him to tell me what's on his mind and why he's shying away from getting married."

"Bethany, he's not ready, and he doesn't want to get into that excruciating conversation where he has to tell you so. It's hard to tell someone you don't want to marry them—even if he's just saying he doesn't want to get married *yet*. It hurts people's feelings. Paul doesn't want to hurt your feelings, so he's taking the easy way out."

"You think this is easy?" Bethany cried.

"No, of course not. But as far as he's concerned, it's easier than the talk you want to have."

"So what am I supposed to do? He hasn't even returned my calls for the past week."

"First of all, stop trying to back him into a corner and force him to talk. That's causing a huge rift between the two of you," I said. "Second, I need to ask you an important question, Bethany, and I need you to think seriously about it before you answer."

"Okay," Bethany replied cautiously.

"Do you want to marry Paul?"

Without hesitation, she cried, "Yes! Of course! That's why I'm calling you."

"No, remember what I said. Think about your answer. Do *you* want to marry Paul? Not does your mother want you to marry him or do your sisters expect you to marry him. But do *you* want to marry him?"

There was silence on the other end of the phone. I knew Bethany was thinking about a question she'd never considered before.

"Let's try something else," I suggested after a moment. "Why don't you tell me why you want to marry Paul? Why did you fall in love with him? What's unique about him that makes you want to spend your life by his side?"

"Um, well, he's really good-looking."

"There are lots of good-looking men in the world. The serial killer Ted Bundy was good-looking, but you wouldn't want to marry him," I pointed out.

"Paul's funny. When he and his friends get together, they're hilarious."

"You're not marrying his friends. You're marrying Paul. He's the one you'll have to come home to every night for the rest of your life."

Bethany paused again before saying, "Wow, you make marriage sound so final."

"It is final. Or at least it's supposed to be. If you're not ready for that, then maybe you're looking to get married for the wrong reasons."

"So you think maybe Paul and I are in the same boat? That we both need some time?" Bethany mused. She was silent for a moment, thinking. Then she blew out another sigh and said, "And I had to go and screw everything up by badgering him to have 'the talk.' What do I do now? Can I fix this?"

"I feel that you can. Paul loves you very much. Just because he's not ready to get married right away doesn't mean he doesn't love you. You're both young and in school. Give yourselves some time. And in the meantime, my advice is to send him a joke."

"A joke?" Bethany repeated.

"That's right. Lighten things up. It'll set a better tone for your relationship and show him that he can communicate with you without being dragged into an unpleasant confrontation."

When Bethany asked me, "What kind of joke should I send him?" I knew she was on the right track. I suggested my tried-and-true dick-tater joke (see chapter 6), and she laughed.

"That's just the kind of joke Paul will like, Louise, but do you really think something so simple will work? I'm worried he still won't want to talk to me."

"Trust me," I told her. "He'll be relieved to hear something from you besides how unhappy you are."

Bethany called me the next day to say that she had texted Paul a joke at 2:59 pm, which was right before he got out of class. At 3:01 her phone rang. It was Paul.

## LESSONS LEARNED

A man will never call if he expects to be dragged into a heavy "relationship" conversation that he doesn't want to have. From his perspective, what good could possibly come from that discussion? Either he'll get sucked into doing something he doesn't want to do (i.e., get married), or you'll get upset, or the two of you might even break up. Where's the upside for him? Consider why he's avoiding a particular conversation with you, and open your mind to the possibility that maybe he's right to avoid it.

### Words of Wisdom

"If you want to make God laugh, tell him about your plans."
~Woody Allen

## EVA AND ZACK

Eva had been a client of mine for over two years. She called me one evening when she couldn't sleep and was particularly sad over the recent loss of her boyfriend, Ezra, in a car accident. We had an instant connection, and she started calling me whenever she missed her boyfriend. She had loved him deeply and was having a difficult time getting over losing him. One night, after another of our long, late-night talks, she told me she was ready to move on.

"I know I'll see Ezra again one day. Love never dies," she said, with peace finally in her voice.

Eva called again a few months later to tell me about a guy she had met named Zack.

"Wow, Louise, he's great. He's funny and sweet and just makes me laugh. I never expected to meet someone so great in the frozen food section at the grocery store." As Eva gave me details about their first meeting, she giggled like a teenager. It was wonderful to hear her happy after mourning the loss of Ezra for so long.

As Eva talked, I laid my cards on the table. The cards weren't very clear, but they did show some deception. Zack was definitely hiding something. As I frowned at the cards, I felt a sudden flash of understanding: there was another woman in Zack's life, someone he was seriously involved with.

That detail was the last thing I wanted to see. After all the sadness Eva had endured, she was finally feeling happy again, and I didn't want to burst her bubble. Still, I had to tell her what I saw.

"Eva, I hate to say this, but the cards are showing that Zack's deceptive. I think he has another woman in his life. Maybe she's a fiancée or even a wife," I told her gently.

"That can't be, Louise! No, I don't believe it."

"I'm sorry, but that's what I see and feel."

"Well, I don't think it's true. You could be wrong. Haven't you always told me psychic predictions aren't 100 percent? I love you, Louise, but this time you're wrong." Eva spoke to me sweetly like she always did, but there was an angry edge to her words. She was upset that I'd questioned Zack's honesty.

I warned Eva to proceed cautiously with Zack and to follow her own intuition if something didn't sound right. I was convinced that he couldn't be trusted, but there wasn't anything I could say to make Eva believe me.

After this conversation, I heard less often from Eva. She didn't like my unyielding belief that Zack was involved with someone else and lying to her. She just didn't want to hear it. Then, several months later, I got a call from a very upset Eva.

"Louise," she said, crying, "you were right!"

"What happened?" I asked. "Are you all right?"

"Well," she began with a sniffle, "Zack asked me to marry him. Of course I said yes. I mean, I was crazy about him. We didn't want a big wedding, though, so we were just going to go to city hall. It sounded so romantic—just running away together like that."

"So did the two of you get married, then?" I asked.

"No. Every week we were going to take Friday off work to go do it, but every week he had a new excuse and changed the date. Zack travels a lot on business, so it was really hard to set a definite date, but he told me he couldn't wait to marry me. In the meantime, I was busy painting and decorating the new apartment we were going to move into. I even bought some new furniture.

"Anyway, one day my phone rang. It was a woman telling me that the guy I was going out with was married and had two kids. She wouldn't tell me who she was, but she told me that Zack had given me a fake last name. Then she hung up on me."

A flood of psychic flashes passed through my mind. "I feel she was a friend of Zack's family who knows a friend of yours," I said.

"That explains how the woman found me," Eva said. Then she continued, "I was supposed to see Zack that night at the new apartment. He had been out of town but was coming to the apartment right from the airport. I was there waiting for him.

"As soon as he walked in the door, I asked him point blank if he was married and had two kids. He didn't say a word. He just turned on his heel, dashed out of the apartment, and disappeared into the night. I haven't seen or heard from him since." Eva sounded angry now and had stopped crying.

"That was your answer," I told her.

"What a lying, cowardly bastard," she said in disgust. "Can you believe I was going to marry that sleaze?"

I encouraged Eva to go to a lawyer to seek monetary compensation from Zack for the money she had lost on the apartment deposit, furniture, painting, and decorating expenses. She agreed and sounded upbeat when we disconnected that night.

After that, Eva checked in regularly with updates. She had followed my advice and sought help from her cousin, who was an attorney. When Zack was faced with the prospect of a legal battle and his wife finding out what he'd done, he made a generous monetary offer. Eva accepted and took her cousin out for dinner to celebrate. While they were out, they ran into one of the other lawyers at her cousin's firm. His name was Larry, and there was an immediate spark between him and Eva. A year later, Eva and Larry the Lawyer stood on a Maui beach at sunset and were married.

## LESSONS LEARNED

Life has many twists and turns. Many times we don't get exactly what we want because it's not good for us. Just because we want something doesn't mean it's part of our destiny. Without rotten Zack coming into Eva's life, she never would have met wonderful Larry. Many of the obstacles, bumps in the road, and detours that we experience in our lives are really leading us to the place where we're supposed to be. Eva understood this when she called me after returning from her Hawaiian honeymoon.

"In a twisted sort of way, I should thank Zack for all the happiness I have now," she said. "I'm not sending him a thank-you note or anything, but it's time to let go of the anger I feel toward him."

### Words of Wisdom

"The very essence of romance is uncertainty."
~Oscar Wilde

## JUST THE FACTS

It's easy to understand why so many of my clients are eager to set a date. A wedding celebration is important. It's the public acknowledgment of a new family being created and a change in social status for the bride and groom. Men and women have been getting married in cultures around the world for millennia, so it's not surprising that a wide variety of wedding traditions have evolved. Everything from the color of the bride's clothing to foods eaten by the happy couple has symbolic meaning and a tradition behind it.

The white wedding gown favored by many modern Western brides became popular in the nineteenth and twentieth centuries as a way to demonstrate the wealth of the bride's family and the bride's purity. In medieval times, the color blue represented purity, so brides often wore an item of blue clothing. It's believed that this is the origin of the Western tradition of brides wearing "something blue" during a wedding ceremony. The color red is often worn by brides in both China and India, although for different reasons. In China, red symbolizes good luck, while for Indians it symbolizes fertility.

Religious rituals performed during wedding ceremonies hold important meanings that can date back centuries. For instance, Catholic couples demonstrate their union by having the bride and groom each use a separate candle to light a third candle, which symbolizes the new family they are creating together. A Jewish bridegroom crushes a wineglass with his foot during his wedding. Some believe that this serves as a reminder of the fundamental change associated with becoming a married couple. In India, both Hindu and Muslim brides have beautiful, intricate designs applied to their hands and feet using a temporary henna dye. This process is called mehndi, and it's typically performed a day or two prior to the wedding. A number of old wives' tales surround the use of mehndi, including one that says darker henna markings predict a closer relationship between the bride and her new husband's mother.

Any good family gathering has to feature plenty of food, so it's no surprise that foods have special significance at weddings. Candied almonds are often given to guests at Greek and Italian weddings to symbolize the sweetness of life. Wedding cakes are eaten in cultures around the world to symbolize fertility. The bride is supposed to have the first bite in order to make sure she gets the benefit of the cake's good fortune. There was even an old English tradition of serving fruitcake at weddings. The number of raisins in the bride's slice of cake was supposed to predict how many children she would have.

There's tremendous diversity among the wedding traditions practiced by different cultures around the world. They have one key element in common, however. All of them emphasize helping a newly united couple start their life together surrounded by family, good luck, and prosperity.

## USING THE PSYCHIC EDGE

Many women talk to me about the intense pressure they get from family members and friends who want them to get married and start a family. Some of these well-meaning family and friends even have a guy all picked out. They refuse to understand when the woman doesn't agree that it's time to settle down.

Unfortunately, many of my clients let themselves become convinced by others that this is the perfect time to get married and this is the perfect guy to marry. At times, my clients have gotten involved in relationships and walked down the aisle with less-than-happy results. Here is a simple exercise to help you determine your true feelings about marriage at this time in your life. The point is to let *you* decide what's best for you, while preventing others from influencing your decision.

Using a magazine or newspaper or the Internet, find a picture of a wedding. Use one from a stranger's wedding so you aren't influenced by your feelings toward the couple. Clip the photo, then relax in a comfortable chair with some soft music playing. Close your eyes and take a few deep breaths, trying to clear your mind. Sit like this for several minutes. Now open your eyes and look at the picture from the wedding.

Quickly, how do you feel? Take note of all the sensations in your body. What's going through your mind? Give yourself some time to identify your thoughts and feelings. Is this scenario appealing to you? Do you envy the bride? Do you think this is the best day of her life? Do you think she's making a mistake? There are no wrong or right answers. Repeat this exercise as many times as you like, but wait at least ten minutes before doing it again.

Next time your friends or family members start talking to you about your wedding plans, remember those thoughts and feelings that emerged when you did the exercise. You'll be surprised at the clarity that can be brought about by doing this. In no time you'll have a clearer idea of what you want, not what others want for you.

## CHAPTER 13

# Commitment, Part Three: What If We Disagree about Having Kids?

People have children for a variety of reasons. Some of these reasons are better than others. Some are downright lousy. So when a client calls me to say that she and/or her significant other wants to have a baby, I always try to get to the underlying reasons behind that decision. And sometimes the answer is unexpected.

### Words of Wisdom

"There is only one pretty child in the world,
and every mother has it."
~Chinese proverb

### NATALIE AND LESHAUN

"He wants kids!" Natalie cried in exasperation. "Do you believe that?"

I was taken aback. Usually my clients are pleased when the men in their lives want to make such a major commitment.

"Hello, Natalie, it's good to hear from you," I said as I shuffled my Tarot deck. "It sounds like you've got some big things happening in your life."

"Do I ever," she groaned. "Do you remember that guy I told you about a few months ago when I called? His name's LeShaun? He's a plumber."

"Yes. You've been together with him for over a year now, haven't you?"

"It was a year last month. On our anniversary I brought up the idea of getting married. He's always over at my place anyway. Why should we keep paying for two houses?"

"And what did he say?" I asked, even though I could see from the cards that Natalie didn't get the answer she wanted.

"He said he needed to think about it. Okay, fine, so think. Then he didn't bring it up again, so I had to. Last night while we were driving home from dinner, I asked if he'd thought about what we'd discussed. And that's when he said it."

"That he wants kids," I supplied.

"Yes! Do you believe him?"

The cards showed me that there were already children in the picture, so I asked Natalie, "Do you want kids?"

"Not any new ones. I have three. One's in college, one's in the Marines, and the youngest is in eighth grade. I love 'em and all, but I'm exhausted. No way am I starting that nonsense again. My uterus is officially closed for business."

"And did you talk about children with LeShaun before?" I asked.

"It never came up. I mean, the guy's over fifty and never had kids back when he was married. Now he's dating me, and I haven't made any secret of the fact that I'm forty-five years old. Seriously, who dates a woman in her mid-forties if he wants to have babies?"

I laid out more cards in order to get a bigger picture of the situation. The cards clearly showed deception on LeShaun's part.

"Natalie, I don't like what I see here in the cards." I hesitated before continuing.

"Go ahead, I can take it," she said with a sigh.

"Well, I don't see anything about him wanting to have kids. Saying that he wants kids is just an excuse to make you not want to marry him. I think he likes the relationship exactly the way it is. You have your house; he has his. There are no responsibilities. The last thing this guy wants is responsibilities, especially the kind that come with young children."

"Are you sure, Louise?" Natalie asked doubtfully. "He sounded so committed to the idea of kids."

"I'll tell you what to do if you want to be sure I'm right. Why don't you tell him that you've thought about it and you'd love to have kids with him—after you get married, of course. I predict that LeShaun will find himself a new excuse in record time."

A week later, Natalie called me back to say that she had done exactly what I had told her to do.

"Boy, were you right!" she exclaimed. "As soon as I told LeShaun that I wanted to have babies, he got all nervous and told me he had thought about it and decided that over fifty was too old for him to become a father. He was afraid of what might happen to his children if he didn't live long enough to help them grow up. What a crock!" Natalie spat.

The problem was that Natalie still loved LeShaun and still wanted to marry him, but she didn't like his excuses and dishonesty. She asked me if there was anything she could do to get him to come around to her way of thinking.

I closed my eyes and concentrated for a moment; suddenly the image of a calendar passed through my mind. It gave me the answer Natalie needed.

"You told me that LeShaun is always over at your house," I said. "Why don't you cut down his visits to about 25 percent of what they are now? If he's usually over at your house every night of the week, let him come over only once or twice. If he complains, tell him you don't think it's good for your kids to watch their mom 'shack up' with some guy."

"Which is actually true," Natalie admitted. "It's bothered me that I'm not setting a good example for marriage and family. I don't want my kids to settle for less than the whole package in their relationships."

"I think he'll come around if he can't be with you all the time. Let him see for himself how much he'll miss you."

"What if he doesn't miss me?" Natalie asked nervously.

"Don't worry, he will. LeShaun loves you, but he wants all the benefits of a great relationship without any of the responsibility. And that's not an option. It might work for him right now, but it's not what you need."

It took two months of limiting the time that LeShaun could spend at Natalie's house before he broke down and suggested that they get married. He honestly told her that he needed her in his life and was lonely without her and her family.

"He was so sweet," Natalie said tearfully when she called me with the news of their upcoming marriage.

She also giggled and told me that LeShaun didn't want her to take birth control pills at her age anymore because of the health risks, so he had made an appointment with the doctor to get a vasectomy.

## LESSONS LEARNED

The excuse LeShaun used about wanting children was merely a smokescreen to avoid commitment. He wanted to be with Natalie, but he wouldn't admit it to himself, so he made excuses.

Many people are guilty of this type of ploy, some consciously, others unconsciously. In all cases, when someone calls their bluff, as Natalie did, a new excuse rears its ugly head. In the end, no one is fooled, and running away from the real issue only blocks them from having what they really crave deep down. Ideally, we should be aware of what we want and not allow ourselves to make excuses out of fear. That's the only way to open the door to the happiness that we all desire in life.

### Words of Wisdom

"Love is only a dirty trick played on us
to achieve continuation of the species."
~W. Somerset Maugham

## JUST THE FACTS

What could you do with $400,000? Travel around the world? Maybe buy a penthouse condo? A Lamborghini? Or you could raise one child.

There are plenty of good reasons to have children, including love, companionship, and the opportunity to buy those adorable little footy pajamas. But no matter how many benefits there are to parenthood, there also are negatives. New parents quickly clue in to the lack of sleep, the complete loss of freedom, and, of course, the sheer expense.

According to a 2011 article in *CNN Money*, "The Rising Cost of Raising a Child," the cost of raising a child from birth through age eighteen was about $227,000 in 2010. That was an increase of 40 percent since 2000. This number assumes the child is in a middle-class family with two parents, and it doesn't even include college. What it does include is food, clothing, education, housing, insurance, medical care, and, presumably, an infinite supply of the latest video games and iPhones.

In addition to the $227,000 that CNN calculated, there are plenty of other costs associated with raising a child. In 2010 the average cost of tuition and fees at a private college was over $25,000 per year. That's $100,000 for four years, not to mention room and board and books. And when your little darling decides to get hitched, the average U.S. wedding cost about $25,000 in 2010.

There are plenty of expenses that sneak up on first-time parents. Childcare, for instance. Few parents realize that the cost of full-time childcare can exceed $1,000 a month. That's more than the cost of tuition at many state universities. If you want to have two children, plan to pay more for their combined childcare than many people pay for rent.

Having trouble getting pregnant? Tack on at least $10,000 to your child-related costs to pay for a round of in-vitro fertilization treatments or potentially tens of thousands of dollars to arrange a private adoption.

If you add up all the expenses associated with raising one child, you will arrive at approximately $400,000. Certainly this calculation isn't meant to dissuade anyone from having children. But before you jump in with both feet—or both ovaries, as the case may be—you should know what you're getting yourself into. And then go ahead and make a rash, emotional decision anyway, because that's what most of us do when it comes to starting a family.

## Words of Wisdom

"Children are a great comfort in your old age
—and they help you reach it faster, too."
~Lionel Kauffman

## MELANIE AND HARLEY

"Louise, please, you have to help me! I don't know what to do," Melanie pleaded.

"Melanie, before you tell me what's wrong, I know that whatever the problem is, you'll be able to work it out. Everything will be all right." I wanted to reassure her because I could feel how upset she was. After years of talking to hysterical clients, I knew that we wouldn't make any progress during a reading until she calmed down and was ready to listen to reason.

"I hope you're right, Louise," she said with a sob.

Melanie had been calling me off and on for over two years. She was dating a wonderful guy named Harley. He was a racecar driver and had a very exciting career. They had talked about marriage, but they had one big problem: Melanie wanted kids, but Harley didn't.

Harley came from a large family and said he loved kids. He was crazy about his nieces and nephews, but he said that having them in his life was enough. He was able to come and go as his schedule allowed and didn't feel guilty if he missed a birthday party or holiday. He knew that his own children would be a much bigger responsibility, and he didn't want to be tied down like that. Melanie, on the other hand, came from a small family and relished the idea of one day having her own children. She and Harley agreed to disagree about children but had stopped talking about marriage. They stayed together, though, because they were in love and truly enjoyed spending time together.

"Louise, I'm pregnant," Melanie announced. "I don't know how this could have happened. We're always so careful about using protection."

I could feel that Melanie was conflicted. On the one hand, she was extremely anxious about her situation, but she was also thrilled to be carrying the baby she had always wanted.

"Congratulations!" I said. "Melanie, believe me, everything is going to be fine. The cards show me that in your heart, you're very happy. Your intuition is right. Having this baby is an event you should celebrate."

"My God, you're right! I was shocked at first, then I loved the idea, but now I'm afraid Harley will think I did it on purpose and leave me."

As she talked, I studied my Tarot cards. It was obvious that she still hadn't told him.

"I feel that you need to tell Harley as soon as possible. Marriage is in the cards for you two," I told her with certainty.

Then I added something that she needed to be prepared for. "When you first tell Harley, he might seem less than enthusiastic. Don't let that upset you. After a few days, he'll grow to love the idea, just like you do. He'll make a great father, better than many men who say they want kids. And don't worry, I'm confident that everything will work out for all three of you."

In spite of her fears about Harley's reaction, Melanie took my advice and told him that night. She told me later that he started huffing and puffing, and she thought he was going to have a heart attack. He didn't say much, but left quickly and promised he'd call her in a few days. Melanie was devastated. Over the course of the next three days, she called me multiple times to ask if I saw anything changing. Was it possible that I'd been wrong the first time and Harley was out of her life forever? Every time she called, I reassured her that everything was moving the way it should. There was no need for her to worry.

Harley showed up at Melanie's door four days later with a sheepish grin on his face. He had spent the time talking to members of his large extended family. They were all excited about the news and couldn't wait to welcome another baby into the fold. They had teased Harley and said, "It's about time!" and "Will a baby car seat fit in your dragster?"

"I'm sorry it took me so long to realize how happy I am about starting a family with the woman I love," Harley told Melanie as he slipped an engagement ring on her finger.

## LESSONS LEARNED

A beautiful part of life is that we can change our minds. Sometimes what's right at one point in our journey isn't so right at another point. Life is full of unexpected changes, and some of the things we resisted the most in the past can bring us the most joy now.

Harley thought he didn't want children when he was a young man enjoying his freedom, which was the right choice for him at that time. But later, when he was faced with the prospect of having a baby with Melanie, he came to a deeper understanding of how much family meant to him. In the end, he loved the idea. Through fate's gentle nudge, he learned what was really important.

## Using the Psychic Edge

This activity is a quick and easy method to find some clarity when you're faced with uncertainty. As with most of the activities in this book, this one is ideally performed in a quiet room with no distractions. In times of stress, however, peace and quiet can be luxuries that are in short supply. One of the advantages of this activity is that you can perform it anywhere, and it takes only a second.

Find a dictionary and hold it while thinking about the question that's bothering you. Close your eyes and flip the dictionary open. Read the first word that your eyes fall on.

Interpret the word any way you think is appropriate, then ask yourself the following questions: How does this word relate to my particular situation or question? What kinds of feelings does it spark in me?

Repeat this process several times. You'll be surprised by how often the word you find has relevance to your question or concern. This activity not only sharpens your psychic senses but it also opens your eyes to your unconscious desires.

## CHAPTER 14

# Is There Another Woman?

Is there another woman? I could probably count on one hand the number of clients who have *not* asked me this at least once. Whether they're in a budding relationship, a long-term commitment, or a solid marriage, women can find themselves pondering this question at one time or another. Often my clients have a gut feeling that something is just not right in their relationships. Unfortunately, sometimes they're right. At other times, however, the circumstances that seem to point to another woman are surprising.

## Elizabeth and David

"You really don't think there's another woman, do you?" Elizabeth asked me yet again.

She had been calling me for two months regarding her boyfriend, David. He was a tall, good-looking businessman she had met at a nightclub. They had gotten involved quickly. David took Elizabeth out to fancy restaurants, and they spent weekends together laughing, talking, having great sex, and indulging in decadent breakfasts in bed that lasted for hours. On the downside, David sometimes drank too much and could be dark, moody, and sullen. Some of his behavior also seemed sketchy. For instance, Elizabeth still didn't know where he lived, and he would disappear for a few days at a time, then reappear, saying simply that he'd been "busy." Elizabeth's intuition was telling her something was wrong, and she had called to ask for my psychic advice. Sadly, she didn't want to hear what I really thought.

"Yes, I do think there's someone else. I see it in the cards very clearly," I told her bluntly. I had been trying to convince her for two months that something was wrong. I had been gentle at first, but when that didn't work, I had gotten more forceful in trying to get my point across. Elizabeth needed to take a hard look at her boyfriend's activities.

"He's so sweet. I don't think he could cheat," she said firmly.

"Elizabeth, didn't you call me originally because you suspected there was another woman?"

"Well, yes, but I really didn't think there was anyone else. I was just checking," she said defensively.

"I hope I'm wrong, but you need to do some investigating into this man. I feel something is wrong. It's like he's living a double life."

"A double life? Do you think he's in the Mafia or something?"

"No, I don't think he's in the Mafia," I said with a sigh. "Elizabeth, whatever I tell you about him, I know you won't believe me unless you see it for yourself. I predict that if you do a little detective work, you'll find proof that he's not being honest with you."

Elizabeth was clearly upset, and she was rather gruff when she ended our phone call. I knew that she didn't like what I was telling her, but it was important that she learn more about David's life before she became more deeply involved with him.

It was more than a month before she contacted me again. When she did, her attitude had done an about-face.

"Louise, I was mad at you for telling me that David was a liar, and I'm so sorry," she said.

"That's okay, Elizabeth. Lots of people get mad at me during their readings," I assured her. "More importantly, how have you been?"

"Terrible," she said, sniffling. "I was angry at you and didn't believe you at first, but David kept acting more and more strange, so I figured I would check him out like you told me to. Boy, was I in for a surprise!" Suddenly her tone grew angry as she launched into her story.

One night when David was sleeping off too many cocktails, Elizabeth went through his pockets and found his cell phone. She found sexually explicit text messages from a woman named Roxie. Elizabeth was disgusted and wanted to find out more about this woman who was stealing her boyfriend.

Elizabeth wrote down Roxie's phone number and jumped on her computer to do some Internet research. After a little digging, Elizabeth was stunned to learn that Roxie was a high-priced male transvestite escort. A quick check of the calendar on David's cell phone revealed that on the days when he'd been MIA, he had time blocked off with Roxie's name.

"Yeah, David sure was 'busy' all those times when he went missing," Elizabeth snarled. "Roxie offers his services online at a website that promises 'Satisfaction Guaranteed!' Can you believe it?"

"I'm sorry the truth was so hurtful," I said.

"As soon as I found out, I woke David up and tossed him out of my house. He barely had time to put pants on that flat ass of his!" Elizabeth was furious, but there was great pain in her voice, too.

"Elizabeth, don't worry," I said. "Things will get better. Someone is coming into your life soon. He'll make you happy, and he'll be an honest, good guy."

Elizabeth heaved a deep sigh. "Oh, I hope you're right, Louise. This whole thing with David has made me wonder whether I'll ever be able to trust anyone again. I mean, a transvestite hooker? Seriously?"

"I know this has been an awful experience, but you've learned from it. Now you know what kinds of signs to be on the lookout for, and you're able to make better decisions. And most importantly, never forget that everything happens for a reason."

## LESSONS LEARNED

Our psychic feelings can help us in so many situations if we only open our minds and listen to them. But time and time again, too many women ignore their intuition and their guys' obvious bad behavior because they want someone to love in their lives. The secret is to expect only the best partner in your life. If you're willing to settle for something less, then that's what you'll be stuck with.

Elizabeth is now in a wonderful relationship with D.J., a man she met shortly after breaking up with David. They took things slow at first and got to know one another. Elizabeth took it as a positive sign when D.J. invited her to his house and cooked her dinner early in their relationship. He

was a little surprised when she asked if he knew any trans-
vestites, but he was quick to assure her that he didn't.

## JUST THE FACTS

After a break-up, women can find themselves lonely and
obsessed by thoughts of their lost love. So what's the best
way to pull out of heartbreak's downward spiral? Different
women take different routes: crawling into bed with the cov-
ers over their heads, drunken all-nighter pity parties with
best friends, or eating a gallon of ice cream straight out of
the tub are all tried-and-true approaches. But some women
have a harder time getting past their sadness, and they might
need something a little stronger. In those cases, guided imagery might be the solution. It's a powerful means of enlisting
the mind to help itself heal.

Guided imagery is a technique in which a person goes
into a relaxed state and produces visual images designed to
address a particular problem. The idea behind it is that the
brain can't tell whether these visual images are real or not, so
it accepts them as fact and orders the body to follow along.
So if a person envisions a tumor shrinking, the body will act
to make it so. There's evidence that everything from cancer
and allergies to anxiety and depression responds to guided
imagery. This technique has also been used by athletes to
enhance physical performance.

In the book *Staying Well with Guided Imagery* by Belleruth Naparstek, the author describes how she successfully uses guided imagery in her psychotherapy practice to help patients address any number of illnesses. One method she recommends is to make an audiotape with restful or healing imagery on it that the patient can listen to regularly. The tape should describe images that help the patient achieve a particular goal. Examples might be imagining blood cells moving freely through a clogged artery in the heart or flu germs being destroyed by a healthy immune system.

Naparstek offers different types of imagery in her book to address physical illness, mental illness, pain, and grief. Researchers have found that guided imagery is also valuable for people who are preparing for an athletic or other type of performance. For instance, a 2010 French study in the *Journal of Sports Sciences*, "Does Motor Imagery Enhance Stretching and Flexibility?," revealed that swimmers who used guided imagery increased their flexibility more than swimmers who didn't employ the technique. It has also helped in such diverse situations as nursing students learning to perform medical procedures and senior citizens seeking to increase their levels of physical activity.

Next time you're mourning the end of a relationship or you're sick with a cold or sweating over a big presentation you have to give at work, take a few minutes to close your eyes, relax, and conjure up positive images. It could be that a vivid imagination is the best medicine.

# MARY AND JOHN

"Mary, I don't feel there's anyone else. As a matter of fact, I think he's going to propose to you soon. I feel John wants to get married," I said.

"Louise, you're usually really good, but can you ask the card people again?" Mary laughed at her joke about my Tarot cards. She had told me that every time she thought of me looking in the cards, she felt the pictures on the Tarot cards were like little people answering back.

I chuckled and laid the cards out again. The answer was the same.

"The card people say the same thing. Your John isn't cheating; he wants to get married."

"I don't understand," she said. "All his actions point toward another woman. What could be going on?"

Mary had been calling me off and on for over three months. Her very attentive boyfriend of two years was not so attentive anymore. He was tired and hard to reach by phone on weekends, and he wouldn't come over any earlier than midnight on Friday and Saturday nights. He said he had to study and do homework for the one night class he was taking during the week at the local community college. When he did show up late on weekend nights, he smelled like an Italian restaurant.

Mary had it in her mind that John must be dating another woman. I, on the other hand, didn't think he was displaying the kind of erratic behavior that cheating men usually engage in. Yes, his schedule had changed, but it was consistent. He wasn't being secretive or sneaking off to take phone calls in private when his cell rang. Plus, when they were together, John had remained as kind, respectful, and loving toward Mary as he had always been. It seemed like something else was going on that didn't involve another woman.

"I feel John really loves you," I assured her. "I also see that he's thinking a lot about money. It feels to me like he has a bill he wants to pay or is concerned about. You're a lucky girl; he's a responsible man."

"Thanks, Louise," Mary said simply before hanging up. I knew she was unconvinced.

Three weeks later, I picked up the phone to Mary's familiar laugh. She sounded happier than I had ever heard her.

"Louise, you and your card people were so right on about everything!" she crowed.

"I'm so glad, but I told you so," I said.

Mary proceeded to tell me all about what had happened with John. She had been distraught one Friday night thinking about him. She was convinced that he wasn't home studying but instead was out with some "skanky ho." Mary decided to sit outside his house and spy on him. She was prepared to stay all evening to watch anyone going in, or follow him if he left.

She told me that she didn't have to wait too long. Within twenty minutes, John came out of his house, hopped into his car, and drove off. Mary was livid as she followed him to an Italian restaurant. Positive he was cheating, she drove up next to him in the parking lot, jumped out of her car, and started yelling at him. When she had shouted herself out and John was able to get a word in, he told her that he had been delivering pizzas on Friday and Saturday nights to earn money to buy her an engagement ring.

"Louise, I felt like the biggest jerk ever! John is such a sweetie, though. He wasn't mad and gave me a big hug. He even brought me inside to introduce me to the restaurant owners," she said. Then she added with a little laugh, "Guess I'll listen to your card people next time."

## LESSONS LEARNED

It's particularly important to be in control of your emotions if you're unsure about the man in your life. Whether you're correct in your suspicions or not, it's a bad idea to let jealousy guide you when it comes to confronting your man. Hopefully your suspicions will turn out to be wrong and your guy isn't cheating, in which case you'll be happy you didn't act like an obsessed lunatic when you broached the subject with him. You'll merely walk away from the discussion feeling foolish, but there won't be any permanent harm done to your relationship. The worst-case scenario is that you rant and rave at him only to find out there's an innocent reason for his behavior—like he's working part-time delivering pizzas so he can buy you an engagement ring. If that happens, you might end up walking away alone, without the man you love.

Mary was lucky that John forgave her for mistrusting him, and she finally got her beautiful engagement ring. Even after that, though, John continued to deliver pizzas. He wanted the extra cash to help pay for their wedding.

### Words of Wisdom

"Our greatest fears lie in anticipation."
~Honoré de Balzac

# Using the Psychic Edge

Heartbreak is an all-too-common side effect of searching for true love. It's bad enough that you don't get to live happily ever after with the man you love, but when you find yourself lonely, depressed, and just plain brokenhearted following a break-up, it's like the universe has heaped insult on top of injury.

Fortunately, you can use guided imagery to pull yourself out of the doldrums and move on to bigger and better things.

Sit in a comfortable chair or lie down. Close your eyes, take a few deep breaths, and relax. When you feel ready, begin to form an image in your mind of the people you care about standing around you—friends, family members, co-workers, your book group, and so on. Add your pets, if you'd like. Insert details to get a clear picture of those closest to you and to help you feel like you're really surrounded by love and compassion.

The people whom you picture physically closest to you should be those who are emotionally closest to you in your life. Allow your intuition to guide you in selecting the people who represent an important part of your life. Your intuition will know.

The man who broke your heart will undoubtedly be among those in your imagination right now. Because he's probably on your mind so much, he'll probably be located very close to you.

Once you have a firm image in your mind, start letting all the other people in your life nudge the man you're trying to forget out of the picture. The ones closest to you can start pushing him back and away from you. Don't move to follow him. Don't reach out for him. Try to turn away and focus on the others in your image. Gradually the man will fall farther and farther away from you, and eventually he'll fade from your view. That's good. Let him go. If you'd like, you can even push someone else up into his place, perhaps another man you know whom you'd like to get closer to or a new puppy you want to adopt.

Whenever you have an opportunity, sit down, relax, breathe, and conjure up this image of the people in your life squeezing the man out of it. As time goes on, you'll find yourself thinking of him less and less often during the day until finally he is no longer getting any of your time or attention.

## CHAPTER 15

# Is Someone Trying to Split Us Up?

Many times your family and friends can see things in the man you're dating that you can't. Listening to what family and friends have to say can be very enlightening. Of course, they tend to be brutally honest when offering their opinions, and a message delivered that way can be hard to accept. Also, sometimes our friends and family see a flaw in our guy that turns them off but isn't really a problem in our eyes. Simply proceed with caution whenever other people get involved in your relationship.

## Words of Wisdom

"Am I not destroying my enemies
when I make friends of them?"
~Abraham Lincoln

## LAURA AND SCOTT

Laura met Scott through a popular online dating site. She told me that there was instant chemistry the moment they met in person. They had been going out for three months when Laura first called me. She immediately launched into a description of how wonderful Scott was.

"He's kind and funny and sweet," she said. "He just told me the other day that when things are better for him financially, he's going to start taking me out. He says he wants to pamper me. Don't you think that's adorable? He can't afford it now, so I usually pay for stuff. He feels bad about it, but I told him not to worry because I really don't mind."

I had been laying out the Tarot cards while Laura was talking, and Scott didn't look like a good guy at all. The word that popped into my mind to describe him was "despicable."

"Laura, I'm sorry, but the cards are negative. I see a money issue here. I'm afraid he might be dishonest." I could also see in the cards that Scott was using her, but I felt it was important to be gentle with this information. Laura was already defensive about him. "I see in the cards that he's going to borrow some money from you."

"Um, he's already asked, Louise," she said. "I just have to wait until I get my bonus at work before I can afford to give it to him."

"So you haven't given him any cash yet?" I verified.

"You sound just like my friends. They don't like him, either, but they've never given him a chance."

"Why don't your friends like him? Do they know he asked you for money?" I asked.

"Yeah, I made the mistake of telling my best friend. She told me I shouldn't give it to him. He needs it for dental work, though. His tooth is killing him, but she doesn't care. And I know he'll pay me back when he can."

I saw something in the cards that struck me as odd, so I laid some more on the table and pondered them. They showed that there was a great deal of anger surrounding this man. I could also tell that if I were too openly critical of Scott, Laura would blame me for not liking him and tune me out entirely. After a moment, I had an idea.

"Laura, why don't you do an Internet search of Scott's name? I feel that if you do, you'll find out a few things that will be helpful. Don't say anything to him about it. Just plug his name into a search engine and see what you get."

"Okay, Louise, I'll do it," she said reluctantly. "But I know everyone's wrong about him. I'll prove it, too, and you'll have to apologize for mistrusting him."

"I'll be overjoyed to apologize if I'm wrong," I told Laura earnestly.

A few days later, Laura called me back. She sounded like she was in shock. It seemed that when she did her Internet search of Scott's name, she found a number of posts on discussion boards and social networking sites from women who had been duped by him. He usually met the women through dating sites, then lied to them, got free dinners and sometimes gifts, and borrowed money that he never paid back. There were six women who had already posted information about him. Laura would have been number seven. And, she learned, during the first couple months that she was going out with him, he was also dating another woman and managed to con her out of $1,500—for dental work, he had told the woman.

When Laura was done telling me what she had learned, I took a deep breath and said, "Laura, I feel that there are even more women out there who are ashamed to reveal what he did to them."

"I think so, too. I'm sorry I didn't believe you at first, and thank you for pointing me in the right direction. I apologized to my friends, too, for not believing them when they said there was something wrong with Scott. All of you saved me a lot of money and misery. I mean, my heart is broken because I thought I had found the right guy, but I'd feel way worse if my heart was broken *and* my bank account was empty."

## Words of Wisdom

"Love your enemies for they tell you your faults."
~*Benjamin Franklin*

### LESSONS LEARNED

I felt very emotional as Laura thanked me. It was gratifying to hear those words. Often, in my line of work, I want to tell my clients, "Don't kill the messenger!" because I take the brunt of their frustration when I have to tell them something they don't want to hear. In this case, Laura had blamed both me and her friends for trying to protect her.

Some women are in such a rush to meet Mr. Right that they have blinders on, and they get angry at anyone who suggests that perhaps the guy they're with isn't as perfect as they think. Laura got upset when I suggested that Scott might not be trustworthy, and she completely blocked out her friends who had offered the same advice. Just because Laura wanted this relationship to be right didn't mean that it was, and ignoring the information she didn't like couldn't change the facts. Love will come when it comes. Turning a blind eye to your better judgment in the rush to fall in love only leads to heartache.

## KATIE AND MIKE

Katie had been going out with Mike for four months, and she was head over heels in love with him. Mike was a tall, quiet, unassuming chemist with piercing blue eyes and a long brown braid running down his back. He had treated Katie well up until a dinner party that the two of them had hosted so they could meet one another's families. The next time Katie saw Mike after the party, he acted sullen. When she asked what was wrong, he refused to talk about it.

"Louise, I think his mother hated me," Katie told me when she called. "Do you think she did? Is that why he's acting so strange?"

As I laid out the cards, I saw nothing to indicate that Mike's mom disliked her. I did, however, feel there was someone or something that was interfering with their relationship.

"Katie, it looks like Mike's mom is okay with you. I do feel that she's the type of woman who's suspicious of people, especially women involved with her son. You'll have to give her time to warm up to you. Other than that, all is well with the mom."

"Well, maybe he's just in a bad mood," Katie said doubtfully. Then she added, "Um, I need to ask you another question."

"Yes, go ahead," I answered, shuffling my cards again.

"My family told me they think Mike looks like a weirdo with that long braid he wears. I told him what they said and asked him to cut it off. Do you think he'll do it for me?"

As I laid out the cards, I immediately saw that they weren't positive. As a matter of fact, it looked like Mike had been insulted by Katie's request.

"Sorry, Katie, but I think the braid is going to stay," I told her. "Also, if you press this issue, it will cause serious problems between the two of you. Now that I'm looking at these cards again, I actually feel that's why Mike has been acting odd. It's not his mother at all. This might sound strange, but the problem is the braid."

"That's ridiculous. You should see that braid. He's always patting it and playing with it. The thing already looks goofy, but he's growing it longer!"

"You can talk to Mike about it, but be warned that you might have to make a choice," I told her. "My feeling is that you can have both him and the braid or you can have neither of them. There's no having one without the other."

"You better believe I'll talk to him about it," she vowed before hanging up.

Katie called me back two weeks later. She said she'd had a long talk with Mike about his hairstyle. It took a full week before he finally explained the whole story behind it. Apparently, Mike believed his braid acted like an antenna or means of communication with the universe. To cut the braid would sever this connection with "them," which was what he called the intelligent powers that guided the universe.

"You were right, Louise. His mother likes me, but he was mad at me for wanting him to cut his hair. He plans on keeping it." She sighed and added, "Mike says he loves me, and if I love him, I have to love his braid." Katie giggled as she said the words.

"Can you live with the braid?" I asked, although I already knew the answer.

"Who am I to come between Mike and the universe?" Katie replied. "He's such a great guy in every other way that I'm not going to let hair stand between us. So what if my family thinks it looks silly? I'm just hoping that one day the universe will start communicating with him in a more normal way, like through his TV or something."

## LESSONS LEARNED

It's wise to listen carefully to others' opinions when it comes to the man you care about, but in the end you must make your own choices. The fact is that you need to decide for yourself what kind of behavior you can live with, because you're the one who will have to live with it. Not your family or your friends, but you. Every day, possibly for the rest of your life. In other words, just because your sister doesn't like your guy's hair, or your friend is put off by his smoking, or your niece is allergic to his cat, at the end of the day, it doesn't matter. What matters is how *you* feel.

### Words of Wisdom

"Always forgive your enemies;
nothing annoys them so much."
~*Oscar Wilde*

## JUST THE FACTS

Throughout this book there have been frequent reminders to listen to your intuition when it comes to matters of the heart. As the stories presented here have shown, your intuition has an understanding that your conscious mind or logic often lacks. Sure, the man you're dating might seem like the perfect guy—he's attractive, attentive, and successful. So why does he seem somehow "off" to you? Or even if you don't see it, what is it about this guy that your friends just don't like? Is it *their* intuition that's warning them away?

At this point you might be wondering whether there's any scientific basis for the concept of intuition. It's such a popular and common idea that it shouldn't come as any surprise that it has attracted the attention of researchers. One believer is *New York Times* columnist David Brooks. In his book *The Social Animal: The Hidden Sources of Love, Character, and Achievement*, Brooks relies on literature from the field of psychology to demonstrate the difference between the conscious mind and the unconscious mind. The conscious mind includes those things that humans are consciously in control of, like picking out which pair of socks to wear or going to get the car's oil changed. But much more is going on beneath the surface in the unconscious realm of our minds, and it's that subconscious that's actually responsible for much of what we feel and do. The nudge that we get from our subconscious can be thought of as intuition.

To demonstrate the influence of the subconscious and intuition, I came up with a couple of examples. You consciously chose socks this morning because you needed to keep your feet warm, but why did you decide to pick the green socks instead of the white? Could it be because you subconsciously remembered that it was the first day of spring? And why did you get the oil changed today of all days? Maybe you saw a woman standing at the side of the road this morning with a broken-down car. The image of another stranded motorist during the morning commute might not have even registered in your conscious mind, but that image resulted in a subconscious reminder of what could happen if you don't take care of your vehicle. As a result, your subconscious mind "directed" you to the repair shop.

Brooks places a great deal of importance on the role of the subconscious in helping people be successful in society. This makes sense in light of his theory that our subconscious mind is constantly gathering and processing information to help us navigate through life. And it stands to reason that what we call intuition could simply be the signal that our subconscious offers to point us in the right direction.

What does all this mean? It means that there's reason to believe that intuition is a very real phenomenon that is important in fostering the success of human societies in general and individuals in particular. Your unconscious needs to be kept under your conscious mind's control because it doesn't always make the best decisions, but it wants you to connect with others in successful relationships. So next time your intuition tickles you and directs you on a path, realize that it's your unconscious mind trying to help out your conscious mind. And listen up.

## USING THE PSYCHIC EDGE

David Brooks' book *The Social Animal* offers an excellent idea for making decisions with the help of the unconscious mind. He suggests flipping a coin. Regardless of whether heads or tails comes up, you're not supposed to simply do what the coin toss says. Instead, ask yourself how you *feel* about the result. For instance, say you're trying to decide whether to go out with a man at work. Heads you say yes, and tails is no. If heads comes up, it doesn't necessarily mean you go out with the guy, but it prompts you to ask yourself how you feel about the coin toss result. Are you disappointed? Relieved? Excited? This activity gives you an opportunity to understand what your unconscious mind wants for you.

Often the decisions facing my clients are too complicated to be made with a simple yes-or-no coin toss. For those cases, I've devised a variation on Brooks' activity. On scraps of paper, write alternate answers or outcomes to a situation. Some of those options will be more appealing to you than others, and some you might feel uncertain about. For example, let's say your problem is "Should I marry Joe?" Write on one piece of paper, "Joe and I are married." Write on another, "I dumped Joe." On another write, "Joe dumped me." On yet another, "Joe and I are waiting one year to get married."

Write down all the possibilities you can think of, then fold them and place them in a bowl. Mix them up. Now close your eyes and think of your question while you reach into the bowl. Pick one of the papers and read it. What's your immediate reaction to the answer you chose?

This exercise can help us feel and recognize our so-called gut reaction to something, which represents what our subconscious or intuition is trying to tell us.

CHAPTER 16

# He Wants Us to Try What?

Humans are very inventive. We're capable of producing great works of technology and art, and we're equally creative when it comes to devising new ways to put our inventions to use. Men in particular seem to enjoy exploring the possibilities of modern technology when it comes to sex. As a result, many women end up calling me with questions that wouldn't have even been imagined a few decades ago.

## JUDY AND JOHN

Judy called me one day to talk about her boyfriend, John. She was crazy about him, but she had a problem with a little habit he seemed to enjoy. Throughout the day, he would snap pictures of his penis with his cell phone and send them to her. He always included little captions to go along with his penis pictures, such as "Just thinking about you" or "Mr. Weiner is waiting to see you." John had plenty of comments to accompany his pictures.

"At first I was shocked," Judy told me, "but then I started liking it. I figure, at least he's thinking about me, right?"

"Judy, your guy isn't unusual. Women don't often talk about it, but many of my clients tell me about the penis pictures their boyfriends and husbands share with them. Men are very proud of their penises," I told her with a chuckle.

"Yeah, I guess they are," she replied. "And having John send me the photos used to be fine, but then one day my phone kept pinging to announce that I had new text messages. It was five penis pictures in a row! I was with my friend Karen, and she peeked over my shoulder to see who was sending me all the texts. I had one of the pictures open and I closed it really fast, but I think she saw what it was. She denied seeing anything, but I think she was just trying to keep me from being embarrassed. Do you think she saw his picture, Louise?" It was clear that Judy was very anxious about what had happened.

"Sorry to say, I do feel that she saw one of the pictures," I replied. "But I also feel that her husband does the same thing as John, so don't worry about it too much. Despite that, I feel you should tell John to stop sending so many pictures. Tell him about your friend Karen seeing the text. That will embarrass him. Tell him one penis picture a day is the limit."

The next time I heard from Judy, she seemed happier. John had listened to her about the pictures and only sent her one photo of his penis daily. He always sent it late at night or early in the morning, but never during the day. This eliminated the danger of someone else seeing it while still letting them share this intimacy that they both enjoyed.

## LESSONS LEARNED

In the past, it wasn't possible to share intimate pictures with each other so easily and quickly. Photos had to be developed by a lab, which increased the likelihood that they might fall into someone else's hands. With modern digital photography, there isn't a middleman between the subject of the photograph and its intended audience, but it's still possible for someone else to accidentally see the pictures. Be respectful, responsible, and cautious, and have fun with your partner. What happens between the two of you should stay between the two of you.

Several months later, Judy called me again to say that things were still going well for her and John. In fact, one evening when she received her nightly photo of John's penis, there was a caption underneath that said, "Mr. Weiner's lonely and needs a Mrs. Weiner." It wasn't exactly the romantic proposal that most women dream of, but it suited Judy just fine.

### Words of Wisdom

"If I had a rose for every time I thought of you,
I'd be picking roses for a lifetime."
~Swedish proverb

## KATHY AND JACK

Kathy called me one day to ask about her best friend's brother, Jack. Jack lived in California and Kathy lived in New York, but after much encouragement from her friend, Kathy started talking to Jack on the phone. Eventually they moved up to video chats via computer. That quickly developed into a standing date every night at 9:00 pm New York time.

"He's incredibly hot," Kathy told me simply.

I shuffled my Tarot cards and laid them out in front of me.

"You say he's hot, but I see that something has upset you," I said.

"Well, yeah, you're right," she admitted with a sigh. "We were video chatting as usual, and I noticed that he didn't have a shirt on. He has this nice muscular chest, so I didn't mind the view. Plus, he's been shirtless during our chats before, and I always figured it was because he's in California and it's hot out there.

"Well, all of a sudden he said to me, 'I'm thirsty. I've got to get something to drink.' Then he stood up, and he was buck naked! He stood about six feet from the camera, drinking a glass of water without a stitch of clothing on. Then he walked back to the computer, sat down, and started talking to me as if nothing had happened."

"Kathy, you realize he did that on purpose, don't you?" I asked. "It wasn't an accident. Actually, I feel he talked to you naked before, but he just never stood up so you could see."

"Really? Yick. What's wrong with this guy?"

"If you think that's icky, you're really not going to like this next part," I warned her. "I feel that he's going to talk to you about getting naked, too. To be honest, I don't get a good feeling about him. I think he's got some sexual issues. I think he enjoys shocking people with his nudity, like an old-fashioned, trench coat–wearing pervert who flashes strangers in the park. This is just the modern version of that."

"But, Louise, he's never talked to me about sex before."

"No, maybe not, but he just showed you the family jewels, and it doesn't get much more sexual than that. I feel he also likes to get naked with women on video chats and engage in sex acts with them that way."

"Well, I'll let you know what happens," Kathy said before hanging up.

It took Kathy only two weeks to call me back with an update on Jack. My reference to him having video-chat sex with other women bothered her so much that she tried to catch him in the act. Using an alias, she contacted him through a social media site. After a brief flirtation, he started sending her suggestive messages. He also asked her if she wanted to meet him in a video chat so they "could have some fun together." Jack described his sexual organs in great detail and said that she "wouldn't be sorry."

The next time Kathy met him in a video chat under her real name, she confronted him about what he was doing. Jack offered no explanation for his behavior and immediately disconnected from her. She hasn't heard from him since.

## LESSONS LEARNED

Kathy was lucky that she learned early in the relationship what Jack was like. It was unfortunate, though, that a guy she thought there might be a future with turned out to be so fundamentally flawed. Modern technology opens the door to meeting new people whom we would otherwise probably never come into contact with. This can be a wonderful thing, but it's important to be careful. Technology also offers perverts, predators, and plain old-fashioned players an even larger pond of victims to fish from. Always be observant, and never ignore your psychic feelings.

### Words of Wisdom

"Everything in the world is about sex except sex.
Sex is about power."
~Oscar Wilde

## Ashley and Clark

Ashley had met Clark through an online dating site six months before she contacted me. They shared many of the same interests and values. Things had gotten so serious between the two of them that they were already talking about a future together. All was well until Clark approached Ashley regarding some classes he wanted to attend with her.

"Louise, I couldn't believe it. He came home all excited one day and said he had something fun planned for the weekend. I thought maybe we were going to see a Broadway show or something. Instead, he told me that he'd enrolled us in a class called 'Bondage and Role Playing 101.' I was so shocked, I didn't know what to say. I wanted to tell him no, but he was so excited about the class that I went with him." Ashley sounded embarrassed as she told me her story.

I took a look into my crystal ball and could feel Ashley's discomfort while she was in the class.

"You didn't like the course, did you?" I asked, closing my eyes to the images that I saw in my crystal.

"It was bizarre. There were ten couples there, all shapes, ages, and sizes. The instructor was very professional, but about fifteen minutes into the class she handed out a paddle to each couple. One partner was supposed to get on all fours, while the other gave them a good spanking. Clark didn't hesitate for a second. He immediately got on all fours." Ashley lowered her voice. "He even told me I wasn't hitting his butt hard enough; he wanted it harder. I was humiliated."

"I feel Clark's been into role playing and spanking, and this was his way of approaching it with you," I told her.

"But, Louise, I thought we had a great sex life. We've got lots of chemistry between us. Why does he like…this?"

"I don't feel there's one answer to your question. He loves intimacy with you, but I also feel he likes to experiment with new things. He also seems to be turned on by a powerful woman, and when you spank him, he's giving you the power."

Ashley giggled and admitted that in the class she had felt uncomfortable among strangers, but when she and Clark went home, they had taken out the paddle again. When she used it in the privacy of their bedroom, she had enjoyed it.

"I think you're right about Clark liking a powerful woman," Ashley told me. "He offered to buy me a leather outfit and boots for the next time I spank him. Do you think he's sick or weird for liking this stuff?"

"No, a lot of people have erotic fantasies, and I feel psychically that role playing and bondage just happen to fascinate Clark," I said. Then I added, "If it's not your cup of tea, there's nothing wrong with that. Although it seems that you had fun experimenting when you got home and you were in private. Maybe the class full of strangers is what bothered you."

"I think you're right, Louise. I did have fun when we were alone," she admitted.

"Just tell Clark no more classes for you. If he wants you to do any research on the subject, you're willing to read a book," I suggested.

## LESSONS LEARNED

Ashley and Clark were able to come to an agreement on experimentation in the bedroom that made them both happy. They both respected each other and were willing to make concessions for the other person's comfort and happiness. After speaking to hundreds of clients, I've found that these important ingredients often separate healthy relationships from those that are doomed to fail. When respect and compromise are combined, the results can be amazing.

"Variety's the very spice of life, That gives it all its flavor."
~*William Cowper*

## JUST THE FACTS

Most women love buying a new outfit or pair of shoes. There's huge satisfaction in sprucing up a tired wardrobe with a new color or style. The change of seasons is always a terrific excuse for a shopping spree that can breathe new life into the same old tired pieces. But what might come as a surprise is that many men enjoy spicing up their closets just as much as women do.

While trying to cater to men's desire for new wardrobe elements, the fashion industry often finds itself in totally uncharted territory regarding both fashion and language. According to a 2011 article in *The Wall Street Journal* (*WSJ*), "Grab Your 'Murse,' Pack a 'Mankini' and Don't Forget the 'Mewelry,'" the fashion industry not only must struggle to develop new pieces to tempt their customers' expanding tastes but also must coin descriptive terms for those groundbreaking men's garments. This is because the words used for women's clothing are simply a turn-off for men who want masculine variations of the same pieces.

Women commonly wear slinky, sexy underpants called "panties," but what if a man wants a male version of the same item? A guy wouldn't want to wear panties, because those are feminine, and it would be embarrassing for him to buy or admit he wears them. As a result, some inventive designers have taken to calling them "man-panties," or "manties." And speaking of revealing men's garments, the *WSJ* article cited an incident on an English beach where a man got in trouble for wearing a skimpy "mankini" that revealed more than the local constables were comfortable with.

In terms of accessories, men need a place to carry their ever-multiplying collection of electronic devices, because there's no way a phone, MP3 player, tablet, and who knows what else will fit in the pockets of even the loosest-fitting men's jeans. So what to do? Certainly don't insult men by giving them a purse, say fashion designers. Instead, how about a "man-purse," or "murse"?

The expanding variety of men's garments has caught the attention of editors at the *Oxford English Dictionary (OED)*. They keep track of the evolving English language and must decide which new words deserve to be made "official" by inclusion in the dictionary. The criteria for the *OED* is that a word has to have been in popular use for at least ten years before it can be classified as a true part of the language.

So keep your eye on the dictionary, because it's only a matter of time before mankini and murse take their rightful place next to other clothing items that at one time satisfied men's taste for something different, like the Nehru jacket and dashiki.

## USING THE PSYCHIC EDGE

Many times we have a question or a decision to make that we can't quite make our minds up about. No matter how hard we try, we can't figure out the right course of action, and we just can't receive anything psychically. In cases like this, I've found that a simple exercise has helped many of my clients.

On a piece of paper, write a question about the problem that's bothering you. For instance, maybe you'd like to suggest that you and your guy try something new in the bedroom, but he's pretty conservative and you don't know how he'll react. Write down a question like, "How can I get Timothy interested in experimentation?" Fold the paper in half and place it under your pillow. Leave it there for a week. Keep a notebook and pen next to your bed, and every morning write down any dreams you had during the night. At the end of the seven days, read all the notes you've taken about your dreams.

During sleep, our psychic abilities are free to flourish without our conscious mind's control. You'll be surprised at the answers and insights your dreams can give you.

SECTION FOUR

# Bad Love

CHAPTER 17

# Should I End It?

Deciding whether it's time to end a relationship can be heart-wrenching. I've talked to clients who have been thinking about leaving their partners for more than a decade yet have never taken action. Other clients jump the gun and end a relationship prematurely, only to regret it later. The important thing to remember is that if you're thinking about ending your romantic relationship, it's likely that your psychic intuition has a hand in your feelings. You wouldn't feel this way if you didn't sense that something wasn't right. But even if something is wrong, attempting a few small changes in a relationship can make the answer to the question "Should I end it?" much clearer.

## ANNMARIE AND JULIAN

By the time she called me, Annmarie sounded like she was completely fed up with her boyfriend, Julian.

"Louise, everything was so great when we started going out. Julian's handsome and funny and he treats me like a queen. At first, I really thought he was 'the one.'"

I pulled a few cards off the top of my Tarot deck and studied them.

"It looks like you were happy together," I told Annmarie. "And I can tell he still cares about you. Why don't you tell me what's gone wrong?"

"He's a crier," Annmarie said simply.

"Excuse me?" I said. "Is that some kind of job?"

"No, I mean he cries. A lot. About everything. It's gotten to the point where I don't want to go out in public with him because I'm afraid he'll embarrass me again by making an ass of himself."

I placed a few more cards on the table. It was clear that Julian was an emotional person, but most of the women I talked to would be grateful to find a man who wasn't afraid to express his feelings.

"When you say Julian cries a lot, could you be more specific?" I asked, hoping to get a clearer picture of exactly what was going on.

"Everything was normal up until our third date. That's when he invited me over to his house so he could cook for me. I was thrilled. I mean, it's rare to find a man who's willing to do that. During dinner, we got to talking about movies and he mentioned that his favorite movie was the cartoon *Up*. I said I'd never seen it, so he popped it into the player. That's the first time I saw him cry. Sure, it was a sad movie, but it was a *cartoon*."

"I've heard that a lot of people got emotional while watching that movie," I commented.

"Right. I heard that, too. But he seemed unusually upset. Still, I let it go. He's a nice guy and a really good cook."

"And he cried again after that third date?"

"Oh, he's like Niagara Falls! TV commercials, sunsets, conversations with his mother. He drove me to the airport because I was going out of town for a long weekend. I thought I'd have to call a cab to drive him home because he was so upset dropping me off. The last straw was a couple weeks ago when I took him to my friend's wedding. He started up when he saw her walking down the aisle, and tears streamed down his face throughout the entire ceremony. The crazy thing was that she's *my* friend! He barely knows these people! The bride's mother was more composed, and she had survived a brain tumor to attend her daughter's wedding."

Annmarie took a deep breath, then added, "Louise, I'm embarrassed to bring Julian out in public anymore. I keep making excuses for why we can't go out with my friends. I don't even want him coming over to my house, because every time he opens his mouth, I'm afraid he'll start weeping, and I'll feel the urge to punch him. I don't want to tell him to bottle up his feelings, but this is ridiculous."

I turned over a few of my cards to make sure I saw the whole picture about Julian. I realized that Annmarie might not like what I was about to say.

"I'm sorry, but what I'm seeing here is that Julian is emotional. Some people just are. Is it possible for him to dial it back a bit? Maybe. I recommend that you talk to him and let him know you're uncomfortable with his behavior."

"And I'll end up hurting his feelings, which will make him cry, right?" Annmarie guessed.

"That's a real possibility. It's also possible that Julian needs therapy. I get a strong feeling that he has a lot of sadness. It might help if he had a professional to talk to."

"So, I'm not being too critical about his behavior?"

"No, from what you've said, it sounds unusual. Also, it's bothering you. You don't want to be with him. That's your intuition telling you that something's wrong. If talking to him and trying to get him some help doesn't work, then your only choice is to walk away."

"And let him cry on someone else's shoulder," Annmarie concluded.

## LESSONS LEARNED

It's possible to have too much of a good thing. Many of my clients call me to complain that the men in their lives are emotionally disconnected. They avoid discussions about their feelings, which of course makes it hard for the women to know where they stand in the relationship. But that doesn't mean constant displays of intense emotion are a good thing, either. If you find yourself in a relationship with someone whom you don't want to spend time with, that's a bad sign. Listen to your intuition to determine if you can—or want to—make it work, or if it's time to move on.

## Words of Wisdom

"A break-up is like a broken mirror.
It is better to leave it broken than hurt yourself to fix it."
~Author unknown

## JUST THE FACTS

"Big boys don't cry." We've all heard this old saying, but is it true? Or is it just some lame attempt for an emotionally stunted father or elementary-school football coach to avoid having to deal with uncomfortable displays of emotion from the boys in his care? Well, there's a research study that suggests big boys with good self-esteem think it's perfectly okay to tear up on occasion.

The study was published in a special section of the American Psychological Association's journal *Psychology of Men and Masculinity* in 2011. For the study, 150 male college football players were told four stories. In the first two stories, a fictitious football player had won a game. The player reacted by getting teary-eyed in the first story and sobbing uncontrollably in the second. Then the researchers changed the story to a losing game, and the player reacted by either tearing up or sobbing uncontrollably.

When the researchers asked the study participants what they thought of the football players' reactions, the response was that getting teary-eyed was a more normal reaction than weeping, whether the game was won or lost. Interestingly, the researchers were able to tie the survey participants' responses to their levels of self-esteem. If a participant had higher self-esteem, he was more likely to think that crying was acceptable for the football player in the stories.

Does that mean that the higher a man's self-esteem is, the more likely he is to feel confident enough to show his emotions publicly? Maybe. There have been a number of successful high-profile men who have let loose with tears in a public forum. For instance, Speaker of the U.S. House of Representatives John Boehner developed a reputation for needing a hanky during emotional public speeches. Such a reputation could raise concerns since the Speaker of the House is third in line to become president of the United States. One has to wonder whether voters would be open to a president who might burst into tears while staring down the president of Russia or China.

It's also interesting to note that the study results clearly indicated a preference for simply tearing up rather than all-out-tears-running-down-the-face weeping. That was true even for men with high self-esteem. So apparently, crying a little is all right under certain circumstances, but it's important to maintain some dignity. Maybe we should revise the old adage to "Big boys do cry, but they don't break down into blubbering masses of sobbing jelly."

## Linda and Elliott

When Linda met Elliott through some mutual friends, it was love at first sight. She told me she felt like she had known him her whole life as they talked late into the night on their first date. Then they went back to her apartment to continue the conversation until the sun came up. In the morning, he left to go back to his apartment. He returned a few hours later with a suitcase, and he never really left. That was six months ago.

"It was so romantic at first, like a movie where two people just instantly know they're meant for each other. But now, I don't know. Things just aren't so great anymore."

"It might be easier if you try to describe exactly what's bothering you," I suggested.

"Well, when we were first together, every night when I came home from work he was waiting for me. We'd cook dinner together, talk, and watch TV. But now things are different. I'm thinking about telling him I need a little space."

As Linda talked to me, I peered into my crystal ball. I could see many images and knew she was leaving something out.

"Linda, I see that Elliott's not a bad guy, and I feel he loves you. So that's a good start. However, I think you have some good reasons to feel differently about your relationship. I think Elliott has started taking you for granted, and he's treating you more like a slave than a partner. You need to have a talk with him."

"Yes! That's exactly right!" Linda cried. She proceeded to explain that she had intentionally left out part of her story because she wanted to see if I could pick up on what had changed in the relationship before she fully opened up to me. She then launched into all the problems that had been making her angry with Elliott.

"Like I said, we used to make dinner together. Now I make dinner when I get home while he lies on the couch, watching TV. He never picks up after himself or anything. We used to do the dishes together, too, but now he just stands up from the table when he's done eating, leaves his dishes sitting there, and flops back down on the couch. He's so lazy, he won't even get up to answer the door or get the laundry when the dryer buzzes. I do everything. His latest thing is that he tells me to do stuff for him. He'll say, 'Linda, make me a sandwich,' or 'Linda, my feet are cold. Go get my socks.' I'm sick of it." She sounded progressively angrier as she detailed her complaints against Elliott. Finally she said, "Louise, should I dump him?"

"I can feel that you haven't talked to him yet about how his behavior bothers you. Why not?"

"Why should I have to?" Linda asked. "He's smart enough to know what's going on."

"He's smart enough about some things, but he's dumb about this," I said. "I feel you need to tell him. Tell him exactly what you expect in your relationship, and tell him that if things don't change, you'll end it. I don't think you can be subtle with him; be blunt. I predict Elliott will change because he's basically a nice guy and he loves you." I was very sure of what I was seeing for her.

"Do you really think he'll change?"

"Absolutely, but only if you tell him what's wrong," I told her. "This is the first relationship he's ever been in that's lasted this long, so he doesn't know how he's supposed to act. It's up to you to help him."

I didn't hear from Linda for almost six months after our conversation. When she did finally call, she was no longer the unhappy girl I had talked to months earlier.

"Louise, you were so right about Elliott," she told me cheerfully.

"I knew it," I said with a chuckle.

"I didn't talk to him right away, but then one night I got home from a really long day at work. The first thing he said to me when I walked in the door was, 'What's for dinner?' That was it; I exploded. Boy, was he shocked. He apologized to me and said that his dad had always expected his mom to do all the housework. As soon as I told him how his behavior made me feel, he felt terrible and swore he'd change. He begged me to give him another chance."

"That sounds promising."

"Oh, it was. And, boy, is he ever making good on the deal! Everything changed. Now he runs my bathwater and puts my robe and slippers on the radiator so they'll get warm for me. We're cooking dinner together again—on the nights when he doesn't cook for me, that is. He's such a sweetie."

"So, when's the wedding?" I asked as I laid out my cards.

"In June," she said with a giggle.

## LESSONS LEARNED

Sometimes all that's necessary to improve a relationship is to speak up, say what you want, and make a few changes. Don't assume that your partner will automatically know what he's doing wrong, because many times he doesn't. By the same token, sometimes you might be the one doing something to jeopardize the relationship, but you'll never know if your man doesn't give you a heads-up. In Linda and Elliott's case, it would have been a shame if she had ended such a special relationship over problems that were easily solved with a little open communication.

### Words of Wisdom

"Experience is merely the name men gave to their mistakes."
~*Oscar Wilde*

## USING THE PSYCHIC EDGE

Are you thinking about dumping your guy, but you're worried that you might regret it later? The fact is there is no guarantee you won't have regrets someday, but that likelihood is reduced when you're certain that your actions are right at the time you take them. This exercise will heighten your sense of psychic awareness and allow you to better understand what your intuition is telling you.

You will need a clear glass of water, blue or green food coloring, an eyedropper, and a candle. Sit at a table in a quiet room. Light the candle and close your eyes. Clear your mind of thoughts and worries, take deep breaths, and get as relaxed as possible. Open your eyes, draw some food coloring into the dropper, and place one drop in your glass of water.

Watch the food coloring take on different shapes as it disperses in the water. Put another drop in the water if you'd like, but no more than three drops.

As you watch the shapes and lines of color in the water, try to describe what you are seeing. Is there a letter, like an initial? A thunderbolt or a celestial body, like the sun? Perhaps you see a part of your significant other's body, such as his eye or lips? Even more importantly, what meanings do those shapes hold for you? How do they make you feel?

Don't let your conscious mind hold you back. Often, the conscious, rational mind suppresses our psychic instincts. Remember, there are no right or wrong answers. The results of this exercise are entirely unique to the individual performing it, and only you can interpret your own images.

## CHAPTER 18

# Does He Want to End It?

Many of my clients call me because they're worried that the man in their life wants to end the relationship. Sometimes it turns out they're right, but other times they just don't feel secure in the relationship. If these women could just be more in tune with their psychic radar, they could avoid a lot of disappointment, heartache, and worry.

## DINA AND NICK

Dina had been talking to me off and on for several months regarding her boyfriend, Nick. The couple had been going out for almost a year. She really cared about him, but he had some peculiar behaviors that she discussed with me. For instance, she thought it was odd that he always toilet-papered the toilet seat in both her house and his own before sitting down.

"My toilet's very clean," Dina told me. "I was insulted and asked him why he had to cover the seat with toilet paper. You know what he said? 'You never know whose butt has been on that seat.' Those were his exact words. Whose butt does he think is on the toilet seat in my house? This isn't exactly the bathroom at Grand Central Station!"

Nick insisted that his socks and underwear be washed separately and folded carefully. They could never touch each other. He also refused to drink out of Dina's glass. Once, she took a sip of his wine, and he poured the whole glass down the drain. She asked me what I thought about Nick and his odd behaviors.

"Well, Dina, I feel that his behaviors aren't just little habits he needs to break. They're a part of him, and I don't think they're going to get any better in the near future. As a matter of fact, I feel there's more he's hiding from you."

Dina insisted that she loved him and was willing to accept his eccentric behavior if she had to. Lately, however, she had been feeling that something wasn't quite right in their relationship. During the last two months, Nick had been acting cool and distant. He wasn't coming over or calling as often as before.

"Louise, do you think he wants to end our relationship?" she asked me.

"Well, I feel he's hiding something. I also feel he's not sure what he wants to do about you. He has feelings for you, but there's someone else he's thinking about. It won't be long and you'll find out for sure." I felt bad about not being able to give Dina more specifics, but sometimes the future isn't clear, especially if Nick himself was filled with uncertainty.

Two weeks later, Dina called me, very upset. She had found out who the other person I saw around Nick was.

"It was Saturday afternoon, and I had talked to Nick earlier that morning. He told me he was going to be home all day doing paperwork. I was out shopping and decided to stop by his place. His car was outside, so I rang the bell. When nobody answered, I thought I'd go around back in case he was working in the garage. As I walked past the sliding glass patio door, I saw Nick run by the window in a black bra and panties." By the tone of her voice, it sounded like Dina was still in shock.

"Oh my God, Louise, I thought I was hallucinating! I stopped and stared, then a huge bald guy wearing nothing but a thong ran by, right behind Nick."

"Dina, I'm so sorry you had to see that," I said. "What did you do?"

"Well, I have a key to the house because I take care of Nick's plants and get his mail when he's on business trips. I never use the key without his permission, but this time I decided to let myself in. I went right to the bedroom, and there was Nick in his ladies' underwear yelling at me to get out of the house. The big bald dude was lying on the bed in his obscene thong, just glaring at me like I was the one doing something wrong."

"I'm very sorry, but it's better for you to know the truth."

"It was the worst moment of my life. Nick screamed that he never wanted to see me again, so I threw his key at him and left. I never thought I'd hear from him, but then he called me two weeks later. Can you believe it, Louise? After something like that, he still thought he had a chance to get back with me," she said in exasperation.

"To be honest, I'm not surprised by his reaction. Nick is a very confused guy," I told her.

"Well, he can go be confused with some other poor sap. I told him to get lost. And I said that the next time he buys himself a bra, he should get one with more padding."

## LESSONS LEARNED

Dina knew in her heart that things weren't right with Nick. She was trying to figure out a way for it to work, but making countless concessions won't salvage a doomed relationship. Sometimes when the man in a woman's life wants to end it, the woman doesn't even realize how lucky she is to be rid of him. In Dina's case, she was too good for Nick, and when he wanted her back, it was too late.

### Words of Wisdom

"I don't miss him; I miss who I thought he was."
~*Author unknown*

## DONNA AND PHILLIP

Donna called me one day to talk about Phillip. She had met him four months earlier at a company Christmas party. He was new at the company, and she immediately fell in love with his blue eyes.

"He has eyes just like Paul Newman! This guy is gorgeous!" she gushed, reminiscing about the moment she met Phillip. "After that, we made a point of seeing each other every day at work and we spent our lunch hour together. Then we started going out every Friday night, too."

While Donna talked, I started laying my Tarot cards on the table in front of me. As I placed each card down, I could feel and see the changes that their relationship was going through.

"I'm sorry to say there seem to be some problems here," I said, interrupting Donna as she started describing Phillip's hot body to me.

"Well, that's why I'm calling you," she said nervously. "Everything was great until a couple weeks ago. That's when he started saying he was busy and didn't have time to see me for lunch every day. We haven't gone out the last two Friday nights, either. Phillip just acts different all of a sudden. Louise, do you think he's going to dump me?" The last sentence sounded so plaintive that I wished I had news that would make her feel better.

"Donna, I don't see that he's planning to dump you, but he does need a little space. Give it to him. I do feel he's telling you the truth when he says he's busy at work and doesn't have as much time as he did before." I paused, then added gently, "I also feel that you have been too needy with him. It's making him uncomfortable. Just give him the space he wants, and things will get back on track."

"I'm too needy? I don't act needy at all! How could he think that?" Donna's tone had jumped from miserable to indignant in record time. "I think Phillip must have someone else he's interested in. That's what I think is going on and why he's treating me differently. Believe me, I'll find out the truth."

"Don't do anything foolish, Donna. You'll regret it if you do," I warned, right before she ended the call. Unfortunately, I knew she wasn't going to listen to me.

A month later, Donna called me, crying. In trying to get to the bottom of Phillip's change in behavior, she had ended up stalking him. She followed him around at work, always popping up "accidentally" in the same vicinity as him. On weekends, she drove by his house often during the day, then at night she sat in her car for hours waiting to see if another woman would show up. She also followed him when he left his house.

"I just had to know what was going on," she explained with a sniffle. "Then, one Saturday afternoon, I followed him to the grocery store. When he came out of the store, he walked right up to my car and tapped on the window. I rolled it down and tried to pretend that my being there was a coincidence, but Phillip told me to stop making excuses. He said he knew what I was doing, and if I didn't stop he was going to call the police. Before he walked away, he asked if I was a mental case. Can you believe he thinks I'm a mental case? Just because I want to be with him?"

"Donna, I know things don't look good. If you had listened to me before and cooled it, things would be different now," I pointed out. I flipped a few Tarot cards and was surprised by what they revealed. "From what I'm seeing, all is not lost. Do you still want to be with him?"

"Yes," she answered simply.

"Don't stalk him anymore. As a matter of fact, avoid him. Wait at least two weeks, then write him a letter apologizing for your actions. Don't ask to see him or get back together, just simply apologize. Then continue to avoid him. I feel in a month or so he will seek you out."

Donna took my advice. It took three months before Donna and Phillip started talking again. Two months after that, they were dating. Phillip told Donna later that he hadn't wanted to end it with her back when she thought he was pulling away. He was afraid that things were going too fast, though, and he needed to slow down.

"We joke about the stalking thing now," she told me. "I don't know why I acted so crazy; it must have been those blue eyes that Phillip has. Did I ever tell you how beautiful Phillip's eyes are?"

## LESSONS LEARNED

Donna was too quick to jump to the conclusion that Phillip wanted to end things. Her tremendous attraction to him made her feel insecure and too needy. The expression "Patience is a virtue" is especially true when it comes to love. Attraction can happen instantly, but love takes time to grow. The last time I heard from Donna, she and Phillip were closer than ever.

## JUST THE FACTS

How do you define "stalking"? Is it stalking if a woman calls her ex-boyfriend drunk on a Saturday night, then hangs up when another woman answers? Is it stalking if she drives past that ex's house several times a day to see whose cars are in the driveway? Is it stalking if she sends him ten text messages a day begging him to call? Where do you draw the line between friendly "keeping in touch" and freaky "scary stalker chick"?

The question of what exactly constitutes stalking is one that law enforcement officials have to answer every day. Some situations are pretty clear-cut. For instance, in 2011 a woman was accused of stalking by Houston police after she allegedly called her ex-boyfriend over one thousand times and e-mailed him more than seven hundred times in three months. In addition to the harassment, police also said she broke windows on her ex's house using a tire iron and a *sword*! In 2010 a San Antonio man was arrested after calling his ex-girlfriend's workplace up to one thousand times per day. And over-the-top stalking behavior isn't limited to the lovelorn in the United States. A woman was arrested in the Netherlands in 2011 for allegedly calling her ex-boyfriend 65,000 times over the course of one year.

According to a 2009 U.S. Department of Justice special report, "Stalking Victimization in the United States," stalking is a frequent problem not just for people in romantic relationships but also among friends, acquaintances, and strangers. It's important to note that the law distinguishes between stalking and harassment. They're essentially the same thing because they both involve unwanted repetitive behaviors such as phone calls, e-mails, following, showing up where the victim will be, and leaving gifts. The primary difference between the two is that victims of stalking report being fearful, while harassment victims do not.

The Department of Justice reported that women are more likely than men to be the victims of stalking, and as a person gets older, his or her likelihood of being stalked goes down. Those who are divorced or separated have higher rates of being stalked than people with other marital statuses, and those with lower income levels are more likely to be stalked than those in higher income brackets. Interestingly, the statistics also showed that only about 30 percent of stalking victims were targeted by their current or former love interest. Another 45 percent of stalking cases were the result of behavior by friends, relatives, or other acquaintances. About 10 percent of cases were caused by strangers, and another 15 percent were perpetrated by someone whose identity was unknown.

The problem of obsessive post-break-up behavior is widely recognized by not only law enforcement officials but also mental health professionals. Psychotherapist Rhonda

Findling's book *Don't Call That Man!: A Survival Guide to Letting Go* offers readers strategies to help them control the overwhelming urge to repeatedly call an ex. For instance, Findling believes that women should force themselves to wait at least two hours if they get the desire to call an ex. Hopefully, in that time something else will take the place of thinking about the man. Also, women should examine why they're so hung up on a particular guy. Perhaps absence has indeed made the heart grow fonder, and he's remembered as being far more perfect than he really is.

## Words of Wisdom

"The definition of insanity is doing the same thing over and over and expecting different results."

~Benjamin Franklin

## USING THE PSYCHIC EDGE

Chapter 17 offered an exercise to improve your psychic awareness using an eyedropper and food coloring in water. In that exercise, the directions included clearing your mind and allowing it to interpret the shapes that were formed in the water by the food coloring. For this chapter, the same exercise is recommended, but with a twist.

Again, you will need a clear glass of water, blue or green food coloring, an eyedropper, and a candle. Sit at a table in a quiet room. Light the candle and close your eyes. Think about a problem that you want an answer to. For instance, perhaps you're wondering whether your boyfriend is planning to break things off with you. Focus on that question, take some deep breaths, and get as comfortable as possible.

Then open your eyes, draw some food coloring into the dropper, and place one drop in your glass of water. Watch the food coloring take on different shapes as it disperses in the water. Put another drop in if you'd like, but no more than three drops.

Think of the shapes as answers to your question. What shapes do you see, and how can they be interpreted in light of the problem that's on your mind? For instance, maybe you see what looks like a rose blooming. You might interpret that as an optimistic sign that your relationship is still in its early stages. Or you might see a flower wilting, which might be a bad sign to you.

As with the exercise in chapter 17, remember that there are no right or wrong answers. The results of this exercise are entirely unique to the individual performing it, and only you can interpret your own images.

## CHAPTER 19

# How Do I Tell Him It's Over?

It's over. You know it. Your friends know it. The maître d' at the restaurant where you had dinner last night knows it. Now it's time to tell him. But how do you go about breaking someone's heart? Also, what do you do when your soon-to-be-ex won't take no for an answer or you fear that he might behave irrationally? As with all the situations in this book, I advise you to listen to your intuition. It won't steer you wrong even when your relationship is on its way to the big Heartbreak Hotel in the sky.

## Words of Wisdom

"Love can sometimes be magic.
But magic can sometimes...just be an illusion."
~Javan

## MARGO AND BURT

Margo called me late one night when her boyfriend, Burt, dropped her off at her apartment after a date. She and Burt had been going out for almost two years, and Margo felt that whatever spark had once existed between them had long since burned out.

"Louise, I don't want to hurt him, but I just don't think I can be with him anymore. He's so boring, he dresses like a slob, and I don't think he's showering regularly. Tonight he stank of body odor. The whole car smelled so bad, I almost got sick," she told me in disgust. "When he kissed me goodnight, his breath smelled like creamed corn."

"I don't blame you for being turned off. Have you talked to him about his hygiene?" I asked her.

"Yes, I have, but he doesn't do anything about it. Today he said that he was running late after his workout at the gym so he didn't have time to shower or change. I offered to let him shower at my place, but he said no because he was hungry and wanted to go get something to eat." Margo groaned, and I could practically see her annoyed eye roll over the phone.

"Actually, it doesn't matter," she continued. "At this point, I don't even care, but I don't want to hurt him. In spite of everything, he's a good guy and we used to have fun together."

As I turned over my Tarot cards, I could see that Burt was in fact a nice guy and was going to make some woman very happy one day, but he wasn't for Margo.

"I see here that it would be best for both of you if you ended it," I told her.

"What do you think is the best way to end it with him? You know, without hurting him any more than I have to."

"I think you should tell him as soon as possible. Tell him to come over to your house. Explain how you feel, but gently. I feel that Burt will understand."

"I just wish I had someone else in my life before I end it with Burt. Whenever I need anything, he's right there for me. Like when my car breaks down or I need help moving," Margo said with a sigh.

"Listen, Margo, you'll never find anyone else if you're always hanging around with Burt. Plus, it's not fair to him if you only keep him around to do odd jobs. You'll find someone later, but it might take six months or a year. In the meantime, you might have to pay a mechanic and a moving company."

Margo called me a few weeks later and told me she had done exactly as I said. Burt came over, the two of them sat down, and she broke up with him. She said he was surprised but didn't seem particularly upset.

"I was a little insulted because he didn't even ask me to reconsider. He just asked if we could still be friends," she told me.

"I think this turned out just right. Burt should never have been anything more than a friend in the first place," I said. "Plus, look on the bright side. I feel that Burt will still be there for you if you need anything, but only as a friend, of course."

"Yeah, I guess," Margo said. Then she added, "You know, when he came over the other day, he was freshly showered and had on the new shirt I gave him for his birthday. He was looking pretty good."

## LESSONS LEARNED

When a woman decides to take the leap and end it with the man in her life, it's not always easy. Many people hold on to a relationship out of convenience, which is what Margo was doing. But convenient isn't good enough when it comes to finding the man of your dreams. Some men in our lives should never move out of the "friend" category, and others should be placed there without hesitation when it becomes clear that there's no romance between you.

Margo and Burt have become much closer now that they're just friends. She has come to consider Burt one of her best friends, and they frequently consult one another for advice about the opposite sex.

## Words of Wisdom

"Promise me you'll never forget me
because if I thought you would, I'd never leave."
~Winnie-the-Pooh

## CARLA AND VINCENT

When I first talked to Carla, she sounded nervous and frightened as she described her boyfriend of one year, Vincent. Carla told me that for the first three months he had been great; he was attentive, kind, and sweet. She had felt a genuine affection for him. Then everything began to change.

Vincent started to call and text her constantly to check up on her. He wouldn't let her go out with her friends. He told her, "You're not going out with those bitches." She eventually had to sneak calls to her friends because he reached the point where he didn't even want her talking to them. Over the last two months, he had started accusing her of looking at other men and having a boyfriend on the side.

"How can I have a boyfriend on the side when Vincent is always with me?" Carla asked me in exasperation.

As she talked, I began peeling Tarot cards off the deck. Things looked very bad for Carla and Vincent, and they were going to get worse. Then she asked me the question that she had really called about.

"Louise, I can't be with him anymore. How do I tell him it's over? I'm afraid of how he's going to take it."

Unlike many of my clients who call for advice on break-ups because they're not sure it's the right thing to do or because they want to let their guy down easy without hurting his feelings, it was clear that Carla had a much more serious concern. She was worried about her own safety.

"Carla, you are so right to end it with him. But you already know that it could be dangerous if you're alone with him when you tell him. Call him on the phone and tell him to stay away from you. Make it clear that you don't want to hear from him again." Then I added, "You were right to listen to your intuition. I feel Vincent might not be a safe person to be around."

"Isn't he going to be madder if I tell him on the phone? I'm a little afraid of him, and I don't want to make things worse," she admitted.

"I feel he's going to be very angry. As a matter of fact, you might have to threaten him with the police," I told her.

"But he *is* the police. He's a policeman."

"All the better because he won't want to risk losing his job if he's arrested. With this guy, you can't be nice to him; you have to act tough. Also, don't agree to let him come over. He'll say he just wants to talk, but that could turn out badly," I warned. Before hanging up, I suggested that Carla might want to invite a friend or two over to give her moral support for the call. I also told her that there are domestic abuse centers around the country that could help her if she wanted to call them for help in handling Vincent.

Carla had to work up the courage to call Vincent and tell him it was over, but the day after she did, she called me to report on their conversation.

"At first, he was shocked when I told him I was breaking up with him. Then he told me I was making a mistake and I shouldn't do anything rash. He asked to come over so we could talk, just like you said he would. But I said no, and that I'd call the police if he showed up here. Then, boy, did he get mad! He started yelling and told me that all women are the same. He shouted, 'You're all bitches! I knew the moment I met you that you're nothing but a nasty whore!'"

"I'm so sorry you had to put up with that abuse," I said.

"Oh, and he was just getting started. Then he began swearing. But after being called a few choice names, I got mad right back at him. I told him that if I ever heard from him again, I'd call the cops and his ass would be fired. That's when he hung up on me."

Of course, that wasn't the last time Carla heard from Vincent. He called her every day, asking her to come back to him and telling her she'd made a huge mistake letting him go. After two weeks, she followed through on her promise and called his sergeant at the police department.

"Whatever his boss said to him must have scared him, because I haven't heard a word from Vincent since. Do you think I've finally heard the last of him?" she asked me one night when she called a few weeks later.

As I looked into my crystal ball, I couldn't see Vincent anymore.

"Carla, I see he's gone now. I feel psychically that he was given a severe warning, and he had enough sense to take it seriously," I told her.

"Thank God," she said with a relieved sigh.

## LESSONS LEARNED

Some men don't want to accept the end of a relationship. Because of the potential for violence or irrational behavior, I always warn my clients that safety is a vital consideration in ending any relationship. In Carla's case, Vincent's controlling and hostile nature would have made it frightening and potentially dangerous to end the relationship face to face. While the telephone might seem like a cold and impersonal way to say goodbye to someone you have been close to, your well-being is far more important than making your ex feel good.

### Words of Wisdom

"Don't wait. The time will never be just right."
~Napoleon Hill

## JUST THE FACTS

Is the letter an endangered species? Back in the day, communicating via a handwritten letter that was stamped and mailed through the U.S. Post Office was a common means of staying in touch with friends and family. Your parents or grandparents might even have a stash of love letters on actual stationery that they exchanged before getting married or during lengthy separations like wartime. In addition, the age-old question "How do I tell him it's over?" could be answered with the infamous "Dear John" letter. This personal, handwritten message got across the point that a former flame was being dumped without an uncomfortable, in-person confrontation.

Today, people around the world rely far more on e-mails and cell phones for their personal communication needs than on the post office. The United Nations telecommunications agency reported that in 2010 there were just under seven billion people in the world. Over two billion of them had access to the Internet, and they used approximately five billion cell phones. It's interesting to note that these technologies barely existed thirty years ago.

This change in how people communicate has spelled trouble for the United States Postal Service. In 2011 the size of their deficit topped $10 billion, according to the 2010 report "Projecting U.S. Mail Volumes to 2020" prepared by the Boston Consulting Group. One of the main causes for this deficit was a reduction in the amount of First Class mail that people are sending. The use of e-mails and texts to communicate with friends and family, not to mention online bill-paying, e-mail marketing, e-cards, and electronic invitations, has potentially catastrophic implications for the post office. Of course, from the public's standpoint, why should they spend money to send mail that will take days to arrive when they can send a message instantaneously for free?

Another sign of changing communication styles is the fact that cursive handwriting is being phased out of the elementary school curriculum in some American public schools. With children practically born with a keyboard or touch screen in their hands, the thinking is that there's little need these days for clear, flowing cursive handwriting. Children can take notes in class on a laptop or tablet, send e-mails or texts to friends and relatives, and complete and submit their homework assignments electronically.

You might not care about the financial problems of the postal service, and you might think it's about time sadistic teachers stopped torturing students by forcing them to learn how to make a cursive capital Q, but there's another reason why our reliance on technology has many people concerned. Warnings from the World Health Organization in 2011 suggested that cellular phones might cause brain cancer. The phones use low-level radiation like that produced by microwave ovens, and placing a phone right next to the ear can result in the brain being exposed to such radiation. There's also some worry that radiation could affect memory and might be particularly dangerous to children whose skulls aren't as thick as those of adults.

If talking on a cell phone is a potential health threat, is texting safer? Not necessarily. A 2011 study out of the School of Public Health at the University of California, Berkeley, "Effects of Exposure to Mobile Phones on Male Reproduction," found that a man's sperm count might decrease if he carries his cell phone in a front pants pocket near his crotch. The remaining sperm could also have mobility problems that might make it more difficult for a couple to get pregnant.

Yes, we all love the convenience of our new technology, but it comes at a price. Is it progress when the quaint "Dear John" letter has morphed into an impersonal "Dear John" e-mail or even an "Im breakn up w/ u" text? And joke all you want about the post office's speed and reliability, but the fact is no one is studying your mail carrier to see if he irradiates people's brains or causes fertility problems along his route.

# Using the Psychic Edge

Still not sure whether you're making the right choice about ending it with your guy? Maybe you want to know how to break the bad news? Try the following activity to bring clarity to your decision making. You might recognize it as a variation on a technique that has traditionally been used to determine the sex of an unborn baby.

1. Think about a question that you have on your mind, such as "Should I break up with Jerry tonight?"

2. Then take two pieces of paper, and write "Yes" on one and "No" on the other.

3. Pretend that the face of a clock is painted on the table in front of you. Place one of the answers you wrote down at the 12:00 o'clock position and the other at the 3:00 o'clock position.

4. Take one of your rings, and run a string or cord through the middle of it. Then tie the ends of the string together.

5. Suspend the ring over the center of the clock by holding the knot between your thumb and forefinger. Make sure the ring hangs at least six inches from your fingers.

6. Close your eyes and concentrate on your question.

7. If the ring starts to swing in an up-and-down direction (between 12 and 6 on a clock), then the 12:00 o'clock answer is your choice. If it swings side to side (between 3 and 9 on a clock), then the 3:00 o'clock answer is your choice.

When you think about the answer you received, how does it make you feel? Do you have a psychic feeling that this answer is correct? Repeat this activity as often as you'd like. It's a powerful way to open up your subconscious mind and get your psychic juices flowing.

## CHAPTER 20

# Will I Ever Find Love Again?

The sadness and disappointment that follow the end of a relationship can be devastating. Many women feel there's no hope that they will ever find love again. Despair might be a natural reaction when one considers all the elements that must fall in line before fireworks can start. Finding someone who's compatible mentally, emotionally, and of course physically is such a tremendous undertaking that it's a miracle anyone ever finds that special someone. Yet they do. It happens to thousands of people every day, and there's love for you, too. It just takes courage to move forward and start again.

## HEIDI AND JOE

Heidi called me late one night. Unable to sleep, she needed someone to talk to, and she reached out to me. Heidi's husband of twenty-three years, Bill, had recently left her for an eighteen-year-old girl who was pregnant with his child. Heidi admitted that things hadn't been great between her and Bill for years, but she never imagined he was involved with their neighbors' teenage daughter.

Now, not only had she lost her husband to a girl less than half her age, but the neighbors glared at Heidi whenever they ran into each other outside, as if it were Heidi's fault that her husband had seduced their child. Heidi was understandably devastated by the situation and felt her life was hopeless. She could see only darkness ahead in her future.

"Louise, Bill broke my heart! He betrayed me in every possible way with a girl who's younger than our son. How could he have done something like that?" Heidi moaned.

"I'm sorry to have to tell you this, Heidi, but I feel that Bill was unfaithful to you in the past as well. The only reason you found out about his infidelity this time was because his girlfriend was pregnant," I said.

"How did you know that? Bill had an affair ten years ago, but he promised me he wouldn't do it again. We stayed together then for the sake of our family, and I thought he was really sorry for what he'd done."

"Bill obviously broke his promise at least once, but just because he wasn't trustworthy doesn't mean all men are. I know you might not believe me, but you'll see. You're going to be much happier without Bill. I feel someone new is coming into your life soon. This time it's destiny. He's your true other half," I told her.

"Oh, Louise, I wish you were right, but there's no hope. It was hard enough attracting a husband when I was in my twenties, but now I can't even imagine any man being interested in me. My stretch marks have stretch marks, and my crow's feet are so deep, they're more like pterodactyl feet. How am I supposed to compete with all those girls in their skinny jeans?"

"Heidi, you listen to me," I said briskly. "I can feel that you're a beautiful woman. No, you're not eighteen anymore, but most decent men don't want a woman whom people mistake for his daughter instead of his date. Just because Bill didn't appreciate all you have to offer doesn't mean that other men won't. The man you're going to end up with will be very lucky—and he'll know it."

"If only that were true. I'm so lonely, and I feel like I'm going to be this way for the rest of my life," she replied miserably.

Heidi called me once a week, usually late at night, to talk out the persistent bitter feelings about her failed marriage. Everywhere she looked in her house were reminders of Bill and their life together, and every Sunday, the neighbors' pregnant daughter stopped by to visit her parents. At least Bill had the decency to not go with her, but the sight of the girl's expanding belly always made Heidi's stomach turn. She found herself staying indoors on Sundays so she wouldn't have to witness the growing evidence of her husband's infidelity. Heidi also confided in me that she had started to avoid looking in mirrors because the lines, wrinkles, and cellulite depressed her and reinforced the belief that no man would ever find her attractive again.

Then one day Heidi called me in the afternoon instead of at night. The cheerfulness in her voice immediately told me that something had changed. She proceeded to describe a man named Joe whom she had met through a mutual friend. Joe was charming and tall, with curly, jet black hair. Heidi told me he owned five franchise restaurants in the city where they both lived.

"On our first date, Joe brought me flowers. I didn't think guys did that anymore," she said.

"As I'm looking at my cards, I see that this is a very special man. I feel he liked you right away, and you have a lot in common," I told her.

"Yes, that's what he said! He told me that when we first met, he loved my smile and my eyes. He even called me beautiful! Do you know how long it's been since a man said that to me?" Heidi sounded nothing like the woman who hid in her house to avoid her neighbors. She sounded confident and very happy.

"And we do have a lot in common," she continued. "Joe had been married for twenty years, but he lost his wife to cancer two years ago. He told me that he just recently decided to start dating."

"This guy is wonderful. I see a bright future for the two of you," I assured her.

From that moment on, Heidi hardly ever mentioned Bill when she called me. She was too busy devoting her time and energy to her relationship with Joe. One of the things they were especially excited about doing together was traveling. They both loved seeing new places, but neither had been able to travel much with their previous spouses. For Joe, his wife had been in fragile health for years while she battled cancer. For Heidi, travel had always been a point of contention between her and Bill because he hated to fly, found hotels disgusting, and didn't like what he referred to as "dealing with foreigners."

"Joe and I are going to Cancun next month. I just got my passport in the mail today, and I'm so excited! I even bought a new bathing suit. Stretch marks be damned, I'm going swimming in the ocean!" she told me laughingly one day.

Then she sighed deeply and added, "You know, I can't believe how miserable I was before and how happy I am now. Things have completely turned around. If someone had told me a year ago that I'd be going to Mexico with my soulmate, I would have asked them what they were drinking."

"Heidi, life is all about change," I told her. "You're living proof of the expression 'It's always darkest before the dawn.'"

## LESSONS LEARNED

Many times we fight against changes that occur in our lives, but we wouldn't fight if we only realized that those changes were leading us to a better path. Heidi had known for years that her relationship with Bill left something to be desired, but she never considered changing it. She didn't realize that there was something far better out there for her. But then when circumstances forced her to make a change, she resisted. If she had only known that someone as wonderful as Joe was waiting right around the corner for her, she would have waved goodbye to Bill with a smile on her face and a song in her heart.

For everyone, no matter the situation, true love can be just around the corner. We simply have to work up the courage to turn that corner. As Heidi discovered, no matter how bleak things might seem, there's always hope. As of this writing, Heidi and Joe had recently celebrated their first wedding anniversary. In Paris.

### Words of Wisdom

"Every end is a new beginning."
~*Proverb*

# Just the Facts

Everyone wants others to find them attractive, which explains why billions of dollars are spent annually in the United States on makeup, fashionable clothing, and personal care products. Heidi in the previous story was miserable because she saw only her physical flaws and believed that they made her unattractive and unlovable. But are attractive people really any better off than average- or below-average-looking people? Researchers have asked the same question and arrived at some interesting results.

Economists at the University of Texas at Austin wanted to know whether attractive people are any happier than their less attractive counterparts. In 2011 economists Daniel Hamermesh and Jason Abrevaya studied survey data from a number of other researchers and found that society's pretty people really are happier. They also make more money and marry more attractive spouses, who themselves tend to be higher earners. In other words, being attractive carries a lot of advantages. The researchers also found that being attractive played a bigger part in women's happiness than men's.

Of course, this research begs the question: How is attractiveness measured? The old saying "Beauty is in the eye of the beholder" suggests that we don't all find the same things attractive. The truth of that statement has certainly been proven by a number of stories in this book. However, for research purposes, it's vital to have objective measures of attractiveness that can be compared among test subjects. That's where facial symmetry comes in. Facial symmetry is a measure of how similar the two sides of a person's face are. Attractive people generally have higher levels of facial symmetry, while those who are viewed as less attractive have bigger differences between the two halves of their faces.

In 2011 *The Wall Street Journal* conducted a study to find out if attractive people with high levels of facial symmetry really are more successful than their less symmetrical peers. The subjects for the study were players on NFL football teams, and the newspaper had a researcher measure the facial symmetry of those players to gauge attractiveness. The players' level of attractiveness was then compared to the teams' win/loss records to measure success, and the results were reported in the article "The NFL's Best-Looking Team."

Some interesting patterns emerged from the comparison. First, the football teams that finished their 2010–11 seasons with the best records tended to be the least attractive, while worse teams were better-looking. Those findings are the opposite of what one would expect based on previous studies. And that wasn't even the most interesting finding. The researcher discovered that overall, NFL players are far more attractive than regular folks, and the players have been getting better-looking over the years. It was also learned that the teams' kickers are generally the most attractive players on a team—even more so than the quarterbacks. An added surprise was that owners and head coaches of NFL teams are also very attractive, as measured by facial symmetry.

Perhaps none of this is a surprise, since being in the NFL at all—whether on a winning or losing team—is the height of success for professional athletes. The irony is that these attractive individuals chose careers where their symmetrical faces are hidden inside helmets every day. Millions of female football fans would doubtless say it's a terrible waste.

# Tammy

Tammy married Troy, her high school sweetheart, shortly after they graduated from college. They enjoyed twelve happy years together until he was diagnosed with pancreatic cancer. After a brave battle, Troy succumbed to the disease and passed on. When Tammy first called me, Troy had been gone for a year.

"I loved Troy so much. He was my best friend, my lover, my rock, but now he's gone," she told me. "I never thought I would be a widow so young. I'm not even thirty-five years old. How do I start over without him?"

I could feel Tammy's pain at losing the love of her life. I felt she was healing, but there was an emptiness inside that would never completely go away.

"Louise, do you think a part of Troy is still around me?" she asked.

I closed my eyes and could feel the warm, loving presence of her husband all around her.

"Yes, I can definitely feel Troy with you. He will always be right at your side," I assured her.

"I had a dream about him last night. He put his arms around me and kissed me. He told me he'd always be with me, but he wanted me to move on. Then I woke up."

"I feel that's what he wants, too," I said. "Why don't you start going out more? Take a trip, take some classes, do things to stay busy. Troy wants you to enjoy life now, just like you did when he was alive."

Tammy called me sporadically over the next six months. She had taken the advice that I—and Troy—had given her. She went out with friends and planned to take a Caribbean cruise with her mother and sister. She was trying to be happy because she knew that's what Troy would have wanted.

"He always tried to make me laugh," she told me more than once. Whenever she spoke about her late husband, there was love and peace in her voice.

When Tammy got back from her cruise, she called and told me about a doctor named Carl. The two of them had met during dinner at the captain's table one evening. Tammy said they'd had a wonderful time together on the ship, and Carl was great to both her and her family.

"He said he's interested in me romantically. He's really open about things like that. No beating around the bush or any games. I like that, but still I told him I want to take it slow and just be friends for now. He lives only a couple of hours away from me, so we're going to see each other again."

"Tammy, as I look in the cards, they show he's a great guy and he really likes you," I told her.

"I agree with the cards. He was lots of fun and seemed like a kind person."

"Would you like me to lay the cards out and see if they show a future for you and Carl?"

"Thanks, but not this time, Louise. Troy was the great love of my life, and I know I'll see him again one day. I'm finally happy and at peace with myself. If it's meant to be, I'll fall in love again someday, and that would be fine. If not, that's good, too. I'm happy just being me," she explained softly.

After a moment's pause, Tammy's tone changed. "Hey, would you do me a favor? Look in those cards of yours and tell me if my sister and I will actually get to go to Tahiti next year. I'm dying to learn to surf."

## LESSONS LEARNED

The greatest peace and happiness in life lie within ourselves. The men we love can add tremendous joy, but real peace comes from inside. We hold the key to our own happiness; we just need to open the door.

## USING THE PSYCHIC EDGE

Meditation is a popular technique that's used around the world for everything from seeking spiritual enlightenment to reducing blood pressure and anxiety. It can also be an important tool for opening the door to the psychic intuition that we all possess.

There are a wide variety of approaches that practitioners of meditation employ, but here is a simple set of instructions that anyone can use without any special training. Give it a try, or feel free to add your own variation. With meditation, you really can't go wrong.

Find a quiet spot in your home. Sit or lie down on a piece of comfortable furniture. Position your body so it feels relaxed. You might want to use the traditional seated lotus pose where your legs are crossed, or you might prefer to lie down on a bed or couch. The important thing is that you can relax.

Close your eyes and take a few deep breaths. After a moment, visualize a place that's beautiful and calm for you— perhaps a beach where you can hear waves crashing against the shore, or a forest with birds chirping in the trees, or any other spot you find peaceful.

Continue to breathe and remain relaxed as you visualize your calm spot. If your mind wanders, that's okay. Just gently pull it back to the location you selected.

Try to do this exercise at least once a day. You can start with five minutes per day and eventually work up to fifteen minutes.

Meditation can relax your body and mind, and when you mentally transport yourself to a tranquil location, it can develop your psychic third eye.

# Conclusion

I received a wedding invitation today. It was from a longtime client of mine named Sydney. The two of us had gotten to know each other during hours of phone calls about Sydney's boyfriend—now fiancé—Kurt. The pair loved each other very much, but it seemed like everything that could go wrong to keep them from happily ever after, did. First, Sydney's employer transferred her to a new city, but by the time she found another job back in her hometown near Kurt, he got word that his National Guard unit was being deployed to Afghanistan. Shortly after he was injured and sent home, Sydney was diagnosed with breast cancer. She recovered while helping Kurt work through his post-traumatic stress disorder (PTSD).

Throughout all the trials, Sydney was on the phone with me, talking out her fears and frustrations. Were she and Kurt really meant to be together? If they were, why was it so hard? When would their troubles finally end?

Every time we talked, I spread Tarot cards on my table and told Sydney the same thing: "The two of you are meant to be. Deep down, you know that. That's why you're still together. You're an example of what true love should be."

And every time I hung up after a conversation with her, I felt blessed, because my work as a psychic advisor enabled me to witness inspirational stories on a daily basis.

Whenever Sydney and Kurt made it past another hurdle together, they grew closer. They had loved each other for years, but leaning on each other and appreciating every moment they shared had strengthened their bond until it was harder than steel. When Sydney was finally declared cancer-free for one year and Kurt's PTSD was under control, they decided they had waited long enough; hence the wedding invitation in my mailbox.

I unsealed the ivory parchment envelope and found the usual contents inside, in addition to a personal note.

*Dear Louise—*

*Kurt and I had to send you an invitation to our wedding. We feel you're as much a part of this special day as any of our friends or family. Your insight and guidance gave me the strength to stay the course through turbulent waters that I sometimes feared would drown us.*

*With your help, Kurt and I have found true love that we know will last a lifetime. Thank you!*

*Love, Sydney*

I smiled as I pulled the RSVP card out of the envelope and reached for a pen.

## TO WRITE TO THE AUTHORS

If you wish to contact the authors or would like more information about this book, please write to the authors in care of Llewellyn Worldwide Ltd. and we will forward your request. Both the authors and publisher appreciate hearing from you and learning of your enjoyment of this book and how it has helped you. Llewellyn Worldwide Ltd. cannot guarantee that every letter written to the authors can be answered, but all will be forwarded. Please write to:

Louise Helene and Kim Osborn Sullivan, PhD
⅍ Llewellyn Worldwide
2143 Wooddale Drive
Woodbury, MN 55125-2989

Please enclose a self-addressed stamped envelope for reply, or $1.00 to cover costs. If outside the U.S.A., enclose an international postal reply coupon.

# GET MORE AT LLEWELLYN.COM

Visit us online to browse hundreds of our books and decks, plus sign up to receive our e-newsletters and exclusive online offers.

- **Free tarot readings • Spell-a-Day • Moon phases**
- **Recipes, spells, and tips • Blogs • Encyclopedia**
- **Author interviews, articles, and upcoming events**

# GET SOCIAL WITH LLEWELLYN

**Find us on Facebook**

www.Facebook.com/LlewellynBooks

Follow us on

www.Twitter.com/Llewellynbooks

# GET BOOKS AT LLEWELLYN

## LLEWELLYN ORDERING INFORMATION

**Order online:** Visit our website at www.llewellyn.com to select your books and place an order on our secure server.

**Order by phone:**
- Call toll free within the U.S. at 1-877-NEW-WRLD (1-877-639-9753)
- Call toll free within Canada at 1-866-NEW-WRLD (1-866-639-9753)
- We accept VISA, MasterCard, and American Express

**Order by mail:**
Send the full price of your order (MN residents add 6.875% sales tax) in U.S. funds, plus postage and handling to: Llewellyn Worldwide, 2143 Wooddale Drive Woodbury, MN 55125-2989

**POSTAGE AND HANDLING**

STANDARD (U.S. & Canada):
(Please allow 12 business days)
$25.00 and under, add $4.00.
$25.01 and over, FREE SHIPPING.

INTERNATIONAL ORDERS (airmail only):
$16.00 for one book, plus $3.00 for each additional book.

Visit us online for more shipping options. Prices subject to change.

## FREE CATALOG!

To order, call
1-877-
NEW-WRLD
ext. 8236
or visit our
website

# Discover *your* Psychic Type

Developing and Using Your Natural Intuition

SHERRIE DILLARD

# Discover Your Psychic Type
## *Developing and Using Your Natural Intuition*
### SHERRIE DILLARD

Intuition and spiritual growth are indelibly linked, according to professional psychic and therapist Sherrie Dillard. Offering a personalized approach to psychic development, this breakthrough guide introduces four different psychic types and explains how to develop the unique spiritual capabilities of each.

Are you a physical, mental, emotional, or spiritual intuitive? Take Dillard's insightful quiz to find out. Discover more about each type's intuitive nature, personality, potential physical weaknesses, and more. There are guided meditations for each kind of intuitive, as well as exercises to hone your psychic skills. Remarkable stories from the author's professional life illustrate the incredible power of intuition and its connection to the spirit world, inner wisdom, and your higher self.

From psychic protection to spirit guides to mystical states, Dillard offers guidance as you evolve toward the final destination of every psychic type: union with the divine.

**978-0-7387-1278-9, 288 pp., 5³⁄₁₆ x 8**　　　　　　　　**$14.95**

DEBRA LYNNE KATZ

THE ART OF
CLAIRVOYANT
READING
&
HEALING

YOU ARE
PSYCHIC

# YOU ARE PSYCHIC
## *The Art of Clairvoyant Reading & Healing*
### DEBRA LYNNE KATZ

Clairvoyance is the ability to see visual information through extrasensory means. It is like watching a movie unfold before your eyes, or dreaming while you are awake. According to Debra Lynne Katz, anyone who can visualize a simple shape or color has basic clairvoyant ability that can be developed.

The only book of its kind that focuses solely on clairvoyance, *You Are Psychic* will provide you with invaluable tools you can use in your everyday life for guidance, healing, protection, manifestation, and creativity.

Katz shares her own time-proven methods, firsthand accounts of clairvoyant readings, and techniques from the best psychic development schools. Psychic readings, healing methods, vision interpretation, and spiritual counseling are covered in this book as well. This practical guide is easy to follow and perfect for anyone interested in developing or strengthening their psychic abilities.

**978-0-7387-0592-7, 336 pp., 6 x 9**                    **$16.95**